α

GARDENING THROUGH THE YEAR

A MONTH BY MONTH GUIDE TO CREATING THE PERFECT GARDEN

GARDENING THROUGH THE YEAR

A MONTH BY MONTH GUIDE TO CREATING THE PERFECT GARDEN

ANTONY ATHA

LifeStyle

To Antonia, Annabella and Araminta who when they were children,
always knew where to find their father

Photography © Collins and Brown
Front Cover and pages 1, 7, and 69 – Digital Stock Professional (Flowers)
Pages 5, 6, 80 and 81 © Corbis/Ludovic Maisant

This edition first published in Great Britain in 1999 by
LifeStyle
An imprint of Parkgate Books
Kiln House, 210 New Kings Road, London SW6 4NZ

© 1999 Parkgate Books

A CIP catalogue record for this book is available from the British Library.

ISBN 1-902617-01-0

Printed and bound in Hong Kong

CONTENTS

GARDENING THROUGH THE YEAR

Gardening is an all-the-year-round occupation: some months and some times of the year are busier than others, but there is always something that has to be done. It is a source of great satisfaction and pleasure, a recurring round of growth and renewal.

Where does the beginner gardener start? All gardeners start with two things: the garden they are faced with, and their own circumstances. Certain questions need to be answered. What is the garden needed for? Is it a play area for young children, or a source of flowers and colour? Is it something just to be endured, or part of the house to be loved and cherished? How much time do you have to devote to the garden, or rather how much time do you want to devote to the garden?

Spring

Summer

Autumn

Winter

THE NEW GARDEN

If you move into a house with an existing garden, I would advise the beginner gardener to think carefully about all the fundamental questions at the outset before making any major changes. Confronted with any existing garden it is a good idea, unless there are a number of obvious things that you have to alter, to wait for a year and see exactly what is in the new plot before starting to change it. To give a simple example, a new garden may contain many bulbs or perennial plants that are not evident in the middle of winter. It is not worth planting new bulbs if you have enough already, quite apart from the fact that you may dig up existing plants if you start in on the garden without knowledge and care.

Nevertheless there are a number of things that you can think about straightaway. The most important is your family circumstances. If you have a young family then the garden will have to act as a playground; young boys and footballs do not mix well with tender shrubs and borders. You may have young children who are no doubt totally reliable and sensible and always do as they are told, or they may take it into their heads to eat the seeds and berries that they find in the garden. If they cannot be schooled to recognise and eat only blackberries and apples, then you will have to make a careful survey of all the plants that could be poisonous if the seeds are eaten. Many gardens contain common plants such as laburnums, lupins, foxgloves and yew that are poisonous, and the red and yellow berries of the yew are particularly attractive, though dangerous. Even if you can trust your own children, they may have friends who have not been brought up not to pick and eat pretty fruit.

THE BASICS OF YOUR GARDEN

After you have answered the questions on page six, the next things to consider are the shape, size, aspect and soil of your garden. The best advice any writer can give to the aspiring gardener is not to try and grow plants that do not suit the conditions you can offer them. If you have the luck to garden on really fertile loam, you are extremely fortunate, but even these ideal conditions do not suit the establishment of a wildflower meadow; wildflowers do better on poor soil where rampant grasses find it more difficult to flourish. Don't try to grow camellias, magnolias and rhododendrons in a sunny garden in East Anglia and don't try to grow tender plants that prefer hot dry conditions, such as cistus and hibiscus, if you garden on the west coast of Scotland. All such attempts are doomed to expensive failure. If you have moved to a new locality make a careful study of the plants that do well locally and then, if you have to create a new garden, concentrate on these plants to start with as they will flourish.

YOUR SOIL

It is important to test your soil to find out how acid or alkaline it is. Some plants prefer one condition, some the other. The ideal soil has a neutral pH of 6.5–7. If you purchase a simple soil testing kit and follow the instructions this will show you the acidity or otherwise of the soil in

THE ASPECT OF YOUR GARDEN

You also have to consider the aspect of the garden. Is it sheltered or open to the winds? Does the prevailing wind affect it? Which direction does it face, north, south, east or west? Is it directly in the sun for most of the day or, if you live in a town, is the garden shaded for much of the time? There are plants that will flourish in shade and don't like too much sun and, again, it makes sense to concentrate on those plants that will grow well in the conditions that you can offer them. For instance, you may be very fond of roses, most roses require at least four hours sunshine a day to flourish but there are a number that will grow in shaded north-facing positions. If you have a shaded garden and want to grow roses, concentrate on those varieties that will tolerate the position you can offer them. All this requires thought, care and study. All the information is available in gardening magazines and books and, failing those, good practical advice can usually be obtained from knowledgeable neighbours.

your garden. This has a direct effect on the plants that will flourish there. You also need to find out the soil type: soils are classified as loamy (the best) to clay, sandy, chalky, peaty or stony. Peaty soil is invariably acid, but clay may be acid or alkaline.

1 **CLAY**

2 **PEAT**

3 **LOAM SOIL**

4 **SANDY SOIL**

3.

4

GARDEN DESIGN

Many gardening books give detailed, often excellent, advice on designing gardens. However, many of the plans that you find in such books operate on the basis that you have a completely uncultivated site to deal with. This is seldom the case. Most gardens already exist in some form or another and it is generally a question of changing or adapting them rather than creating a dream from scratch. Also, many gardens will have one or two features that you want to retain that will affect the final plan and design. The main feature may well be a mature tree that you wish to cherish and the exact design that you can create depends very much on the site, your own wishes and, of course, your budget. Redesigning a garden is an expensive business and you may want to limit the amount that is spent.

Within these limits, the best gardens of all sizes retain some air of mystery. They do not reveal themselves all at once, a journey around a garden should contain a number of surprises, rather like reading a good book where you want to find out what is on the next page.

The rectangular garden

This applies even to the small, plain, town garden with a basic rectangular plot and a patio at the rear of the house. The ambitious gardener could consider planting a low hedge at the end of the patio, lavender if the house faced south, box, fuchsia or potentilla if the back of the house was in shade for much of the day. The lawn can then be shaped to narrow at the far end, to create the illusion of distance, and the end of the garden raised to give a new level. This would make a series of divisions, rooms with different aspects, and give the garden much greater interest than retaining the simple rectangular shape on one level without modification.

The main design elements in any garden are the lawn and the trees. A garden with mature trees has to be designed around them, and most gardeners would have a lawn, even a very small one in a little town garden, as a green patch is restful to the eye in the middle of a dusty town in summer. If you have room, you can always plant a tree to act as a focal point, for even the most compact garden will benefit from a small upright tree.

Wide, shallow plot

PLANTING AND PRUNING

There is no room in a book of this size to go into great detail on these important gardening topics, you have to check them in a gardening encyclopedia. If you are planting a new tree or shrub, dig a large hole, check the soil level on the plant, make sure that the hole is big enough to hold the plant with space to spare, add compost and some bonemeal to the hole, firm the soil in around the roots of the plant with your hands, tread it firm and water thoroughly, especially when the weather is dry.

If you are in doubt about pruning you must consult a specialist book. There are a number of excellent ones available that give full details on how trees and shrubs must be pruned and the correct time of the year for each plant.

If you are a beginner then two things are important. Firstly, try and get the gardening jobs done at the right time of the year. You will end up having to spend much more time doing them if you don't. Secondly, whatever happens, don't worry. Don't worry about plants dying, plants not growing, things done incorrectly. Plants have two options, either they live or they die. If they die they can be replaced.

Gardening has, alas, its own language and serious gardening reference books can be very difficult to read and understand. I have deliberately tried to avoid using technical words in this book. To say 'flowers in a clump on an upright stem' gives most people a better idea of the plant than 'held erect on a corymb of up to 12 flowers' – even if the latter is botanically correct and describes the flowerhead exactly.

I have, however, followed Linnean nomenclature in naming all the plants. This identifies the plant precisely; some plants have several common names, and different common names apply in different parts of the country. The trouble with this is that botanists and professional gardeners are constantly discovering that plants have been classified incorrectly – or that an earlier name exists for a plant. If this happens the earlier name then becomes 'correct' and is used. A recent example would be the common shrub 'Buddleia' that was spelt with an 'i' for years until someone discovered that it had first been written with a 'j' – correctly it is now spelled 'Buddleja'.

Many nurseries and garden centres do not purchase the new edition of *Plant Finder*, the gardener's bible of plant names, each year and may be years out of date. This is no help to the beginner gardener when it comes to identifying or buying particular plants. Where a plant's Latin name is commonly known and has been changed it is customary to add the old name after the correct name, e.g. *Viburnum farreri* syn. *V. fragrans* – syn. = synonymous with.

I have used the technical term genus for a group of plants. To say 'family' would have been easier and probably more understandable but 'family' in plant terms means a larger grouping of plants, one up the scale from a genus. For example both roses (Rosa) and cherries (Prunus) belong to the same plant family, Rosacea.

I have called different plants within a genus 'varieties'. This is technically incorrect but readily understandable.

Within a genus there are 'species' plants, founding fathers of the genus as it were. *Geranium cinereum* and *G. macrorrhizum* are both species of the genus *Geranium* and are correctly written in italics with no capital letter. *G. c.* 'Ballerina' is a cultivar, a cultivated variety of the species *G. cinereum*. There are many, many thousands of cultivars of plants available to the gardener and they are denoted with their name in roman type with capitals within single quotation marks. To make matters even more complicated there are naturally occurring varieties of species e. g. *G. cinereum* var. *subcaulescens*, cultivars of the variety e.g. *G. c.* var. *s.* 'Splendens' and sub-species of the species e.g. *G. asphodeloides* ssp. *sintenisii*.

The other technical term I have used is raceme. This is very commonly used in gardening and means a long tress of flowers, a good example would be wisteria or laburnum flowers dangling down in a long spray – some racemes, however, are upright.

Spring

EARLY SPRING

There is often a slight hiatus when the snowdrops are over, before the daffodils start to flower. Nevertheless, as the days lengthen more plants come into bloom. Blossom appears and the first green leaves begin to show on the branches of the trees. Among the most attractive of the early trees are the cherry, peach and almond blossoms that flower in spring. These trees may all need some protection if spring frosts return as they are so prone to do. This is the time of year when the yellow blossoms of the kerria and first sprigs of forsythia appear, promising the golden summer to follow. The catkins and yellow flowerheads on the twisted hazel, corylus, and corylopsis emerge and the first camellias show their exotic flowers.

Gardeners can look forward to increased activity in the garden. Longer hours of daylight help plants into growth, and there is increasing warmth in the sun. There is, generally, a considerable difference in the temperature between the different parts of the country at this time of year. In the North the weather may well still be bitter and cold, and little can be done in the garden, while in the South warmth returns to the sun and the first annuals can be sown out of doors. As a general rule it is much better to delay any sowing slightly, and it is a good idea to check the soil temperature before sowing seeds. Seeds need a temperature of 7°C (45°F) to germinate, and to be on the safe side it is best to ensure that the soil temperature has reached this for a week before sowing early annuals and vegetables.

Crocus x luteus 'Golden Yellow'

THE FLOWERS AND SHRUBS OF ...

JOBS FOR THE MONTH

The fruit and vegetable garden

- Cut out all old raspberry canes and tie up the new canes if this was not done last autumn.
- Cut down autumn-fruiting raspberries if this was not done last month.
- Sow broad beans, parsnips and early peas, early shallots, and Jerusalem artichokes (if you are brave enough to grow them – they are very invasive).
- If you have cloches, wash and prepare them and sow early carrots and lettuces under them.
- Lift and separate old clumps of rhubarb and plant new crowns that you have purchased.

Garrya elliptica 'James Roof'

Bergenia
(Elephant's ears)
These useful plants, which rejoice in their descriptive common name, flower in early spring and generally have upright clusters of pink to purple flowers. Some varieties are white. The large round leaves often turn brilliant red in the autumn and they are good ground-cover plants for borders and the wilder areas of the garden.

Chaenomeles
(Flowering quince, Japonica)
Often just known as japonica, the flowering or Japanese quince is generally grown as a wall shrub and flowers on bare branches early in spring. The flowers, white, pink or red, according to the variety grown, are followed by edible yellow or red fruit. *C. x superba* 'Crimson and Gold' has particularly striking red flowers with gold centres.

Chimonanthus
(Wintersweet)
Deciduous or evergreen shrubs that have waxy, fragrant flowers in late winter or early spring. Their scent is overpowering and one branch can scent a whole room. The plant is named after the Greek, 'cheimon' meaning winter and 'anthos' meaning flower. They do best if they are grown with the protection of a south-facing wall. *C. praecox* 'Grandiflorus' and 'Luteus' are the two best varieties.

Chionodoxa
(Glory of the snow)
One of the lesser-known bulbs of spring that deserves to be more widely planted. Chionodoxa have delicate star-shaped flowers, generally in shades of blue although some are pink. They self-seed freely.

Crocus
There are crocuses that flower in the autumn but for the majority of gardeners the crocus is a much-loved flower of the spring. There are many varieties, generally white, yellow and purple, and they flower from late winter onwards. The bulbs prefer dry sunny conditions, and the sight of a bed of crocuses stretching their petals open in the sunshine of spring is one of the early pleasures of the gardening year.

early

Iris danfordiae

Cyclamen coum
(Hardy cyclamen)
For the gardener *Cyclamen coum* is the hardy cyclamen that flowers in spring. *C. hederifolium*, often known by its old name of *C. neapolitanum*, flowers in the autumn. These are charming plants with pink, red and white flowers, shaped rather like small, multi-winged bats. They prefer shady, moist conditions and are usually grown under trees.

Forsythia
(Golden bell)
The bright yellow flowers of the forsythia are one of the first signs of spring. They carry masses of yellow flowers on bare branches in advance of green leaves. The shrubs tend to become rather straggly and should be pruned after flowering, if required, to keep them within bounds.

Garrya elliptica
(Silk-tassel bush)
This evergreen shrub or small tree is generally found growing against a wall, as it likes some protection. It is grown for the long grey-green catkins with yellow anthers that appear from late winter to early spring.

Iris
Iris unguicularis, the Algerian Iris, and the bulbous *reticulata* and Juno irises such as *Iris danfordiae* are the early irises that flower from late winter to early spring. There are several species and varieties available, usually in shades of blue and violet. They like some protection from the weather and flower best in a sheltered and sunny position. Divide the plants in the autumn if they become too congested.

19

spring

EARLY SPRING

The flower and shrub garden

- Assuming that the weather is fine enough, clear the lawn, and mow the grass with the cutter blades set at a high level.
- Prune Group 3 clematis. Pruning clematis is a bit complicated, and it is important to note the variety you have bought or try and identify the ones already present in your garden, so that they can be pruned correctly. The easiest are the clematis that flower after the end of June on new wood produced in the current year. These are the Group 3 clematis and include some of the large-flowered varieties, such as 'Jackmanii Superba', 'Hagley Hybrid' and 'Star of India'. Group 3 also includes herbaceous and semi-herbaceous varieties, the *viticella* varieties that flower from July onwards, and some small – flowered varieties, such as the *texensis* hybrids. All these should be cut down to 45 cm (18 in) just above a pair of strong buds in late February-early March.
- Group 2 clematis, large-flowered clematis that flower on old wood in May and June, can be treated as Group 3 clematis, in which case they will flower later and have fewer blooms, or they can be pruned after flowering, shortening the side shoots and cutting out any dead stems.
- Prune wisteria. Cut all lateral shoots back to 2–3 buds.
- Prune hybrid tea and floribunda roses if you have left this until the early spring. Feed all roses after pruning. The best way to prune hybrid tea and floribunda roses is to cut straight across the plant 30–45 cm (12–18 in) above the ground. This looks untidy to start with, but the rose will have more and better flowers than if you prune in the traditional way to an outward-facing bud.
- Prune all shrubs that flower on new wood produced in the coming summer. A number of these can be cut almost to the ground. Shrubs in this class include *Buddleja davidii*, caryopteris, deciduous ceanothus, ceratostigma, hardy fuchsia, perovskia, and romneya. A number of shrubs grown for the colour of their wood in winter are also treated in this way. These include the red-stemmed dogwood, *Cornus alba*, *Cotinus coggygria*, the smoke bush, and the white bramble, *Rubus cockburnianus*.
- Divide up any congested plants in the herbaceous border. Replant the outside of the plant and throw away the centre portion.
- Plant gladioli, galtonia and lily bulbs.
- Sow sweet peas outside in a cold frame .
- Lift and separate snowdrops when they finish flowering.
- Let the foliage of all bulbs die down naturally. Don't mow the grass if it contains leaves, and water the foliage two or three times during the spring with a liquid fertiliser to feed the bulb.
- Don't be tempted to sow too many seeds or do too much work on the herbaceous border in mild periods at this time of year, as there is generally a frost or two still to come.

Leucojum vernum
(Snowflake)
Just like giant snowdrops, some species of snowflakes flower in summer and autumn, but *L. vernum*, the spring snowflake, and its varieties flower in spring. They have charming, bell-shaped, green-tipped flowers.

Magnolia x soulangeana
Magnolias start to flower early in the year and the flowers are much affected by late frosts that may render them brown and unattractive. In years when frosts are absent they are among the most striking of the early flowering shrubs. The most commonly grown are the *soulangeana* hybrids that come in shades of pink and purple to white. The vast majority of magnolias need moist, acid to neutral soil, and there is little point in trying to grow them if you cannot provide these conditions for them.

Pulmonaria
(Lungwort)
These are among the earliest plants to flower in spring. The flowers are funnel-shaped and held on upright stems, usually pink or shades of blue,

although some white varieties are available. Lungworts get their common name from their spotted leaves and make good ground-cover plants. They like some shade.

Viola odorata
(English violet, Sweet violet)
This is one of the small unpretentious spring plants that flowers from late winter onwards. It has very sweet-smelling flowers, usually violet or white. It is better to grow violets in a wild area of the garden where they can spread freely rather than in a formal bed where they may be unappreciated.

Viola tricolor

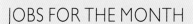

21

JOBS FOR THE MONTH

The greenhouse
- Take cuttings of any bedding plants you have saved from the previous year.
- Sow summer annuals: these include antirrhinums, marguerites, carnations, stocks, phlox, tobacco plants (nicotiana) and lobelia.
- Start tuberous begonias into growth setting them in boxes of sandy soil.
- Sow seeds of any hardy perennials that you plan to plant out later in the year for flowering the following year. These can include dianthus (pinks), delphiniums, lupins, campanula (bellflower) and geums.
- Repot any orchid plants that have become congested – use orchid compost only.

MID SPRING

This is one of the most rewarding and also the busiest times of the year for the gardener. Many of the most beautiful trees and shrubs flower in mid spring and the daffodils and early tulips are in full bloom. Above all there is the fresh green of the young leaves on all the trees as nature comes to life after winter sleep.

Many favourite plants are in flower this month: aubrieta hangs in purple clumps down the walls of cottage gardens, it needs to be cut back after flowering to keep it reasonably tidy; the small flowers of *Anemone blanda* emerge with their long-petalled daisy-like flowerheads; the quince, cydonia, with its pale pink blossoms, and the sweet-smelling yellow broom, cytisus, also flowers as do early tulips. Among favourite shrubs that flower now are *Magnolia stellata*, the star magnolia, *Osmanthus* x *burkwoodii*, with its small white fragrant flowers and the flowering currants or ribes, that can be grown as an informal hedge.

In the kitchen garden much needs to be done – preparing beds and sowing the first crops of the summer and autumn. Do not be in too much of a hurry to sow all the vegetables as a number of them, such as beetroot, French beans and runner beans, need to wait until all danger of frosts has finally passed. Above all the gardener has to pray for no harmful late frosts, rain at night rather than at the weekend, and wind from the south-west.

22

Tulipa clusiana

THE FLOWERS AND SHRUBS OF ...

Choisya ternata

Narcissus 'Peeping Tom'

Amelanchier
(The Snowy Mespilus)
One of the best small trees that you can grow in any garden so long as you have reasonably acid soil. The leaves usually emerge as bronze in the spring, turn dark green and then acquire lovely autumn colours of gold and red at the end of the year. There is the added bonus of long racemes of white flowers, followed by black fruits. A. 'Ballerina' and A. *lamarckii* are two of the more common varieties.

Berberis
(Barberry)
A large genus of shrubs, both evergreen and deciduous, grown for their colourful foliage in autumn and small orange, yellow to red flowers in spring. B. *darwinii*, which has dark orange flowers, is one of the best known varieties.

Camellia
Another large genus of evergreen shrubs with glossy lance-shaped leaves, some of which are fully hardy, some frost tender. They have beautiful flowers that emerge in the spring, generally in shades of pink, although white, red and yellow camellias are also grown. Don't try to grow camellias unless you can offer them at least partial shade and acid

mid

soil. They don't like the early morning sun and spring frosts can damage the flowers so they may need some protection.

Choisya ternata
(Mexican orange blossom)
A useful shrub that can grow too large for a small garden fairly quickly. It is evergreen with attractive dark green leaves, and small white fragrant flowers in spring with a secondary flush in the autumn. The variety 'Sundance' has yellow leaves.

Clematis montana, alpina & macropetala hybrids
These are the earliest clematis that flower from mid-March onwards. *C. montana* is a vigorous climber with small white flowers. There are a number of pink-flowered varieties. *C. alpina* and *C. macropetala* have small, bell-shaped flowers. *C. montana* will eventually need to be cut back hard after flowering otherwise it will outgrow the space allotted to it.

Deutzia
An attractive genus of mainly deciduous shrubs with pink or white flowers that do not grow too quickly or large for the smaller garden. They like sun and may need some protection in cold areas.

Euphorbia
A large and varied genus of plants. The most common garden varieties are *E. characias* ssp. *wulfenii*, a magnificent plant if you have a large enough garden to accommodate it, and *E. amygdaloides* and *E. cyparissias*, that can be grown in smaller borders. The large-flowered varieties prefer full sun. The sap is an irritant and care must be taken when handling the plants.

spring

MID SPRING

JOBS FOR THE MONTH

The flower and shrub garden

- You will have to start mowing the lawn regularly. Apply fertiliser and selective weedkiller.
- Prune winter-flowering shrubs, such as winter jasmine, when they have finished flowering.
- Clip winter-flowering heathers if this has not been done before and prune your roses and clematis if you have not managed to do this already.
- Trim St John's wort (*Hypericum calcynum*) and ivy.
- Feed and mulch all the shrubs and roses if you have not done this before.
- Give the herbaceous border its final tidy and then apply a mulch of garden compost or leaf mould.
- Start staking the plants in the herbaceous border and take root cuttings of delphiniums.
- This is one of the two times in the year when you can make a new lawn, the other is in the autumn. Prepare the site thoroughly, give the ground some time to settle, and either sow grass seed or lay turf (see page 70-71).
- Sow hardy annuals out of doors and plant any perennials or shrubs that you have purchased. Evergreens not planted by mid autumn should not be planted till the middle of spring as cold winds can burn the foliage if the roots are not properly established.
- Plant out sweet peas that you have started off in the greenhouse and plant out the summer bulbs and tubers, gladioli, crocosmia, galtonias and lilies.

Fritillaria meleagris
(Snake's head fritillary)
Originally a native plant, this charming small bulb likes damp conditions and naturalises well in long grass. It may have purple, pink or white flowers in spring. As with all bulbs do not mow the grass until the leaves have died down.

Hyacinthoides
(Bluebell)
Bluebells used to be called endymion, a much more romantic name. They are one of the best plants for spring, flowering slightly later than daffodils, and are best grown in fairly wild conditions as they are invasive and not suited to formal borders.

Hyacinthus
(Hyacinth)
All garden varieties come from *H. orientalis*. Many people grow specially prepared hyacinths for flowering indoors, but they make fine border displays when planted outside.

Muscari
(Grape hyacinth)
Another popular bulb of the spring with its clusters of small blue flowers. *M. armeniacum* and its

Clematis montana 'Odorata'

varieties are the ones most commonly grown. Grape hyacinths spread freely and do best in a semi-wild garden.

Narcissus
(Daffodils and narcissi)
In common parlance, when gardeners talk about daffodils, they mean large-flowered, early flowering bulbs, narcissi are smaller, the flowers are more delicate and they bloom slightly later. This is confusing because the Latin name under which all the bulbs go is narcissus. There are over 60 species of narcissus from which have been developed the thousands of varieties available to the modern gardener. Plant new bulbs as early in September as possible to give them a long growing season and

Anemone coronaria

whatever you do don't buy the mixed bags available cheaply. You will then acquire an ill-assorted mixture of colours all of which flower at slightly different times. It is much better to buy bags of four or five varieties from a reputable supplier and plant them in individual groups. Plant the bulbs deeply and water the plants when they have flowered with liquid fertiliser to build up their strength. Let all the foliage die right down before cutting the grass if you have planted them in a meadow or lawn.

Pieris
Most attractive evergreen shrubs with dark green leaves, they are usually grown for the young leaves that are often bright red in spring. They also have long sprays (panicles)

of pink or white flowers in spring. They like moist, acid soil and partial shade and will not flourish unless you can provide these conditions.

Prunus
(Ornamental cherry)
A large genus of trees and shrubs that are usually grown for their flowers that emerge in spring. These do not last for very long, and are

Muscari armeniacum

JOBS FOR THE MONTH

The fruit and vegetable garden
- Plant new fruit bushes and trees if this has not been done before. If you cannot plant them this month you should wait until the autumn.
- Weed and mulch fruit bushes and strawberry beds.
- Dig over and prepare beds for sowing vegetables and start sowing early vegetables.
- Plant early potatoes. Traditionally, main crop potatoes are planted on Good Friday.
- Plant asparagus crowns if you are planning an asparagus bed.

JOBS FOR THE MONTH

Hints and tips

- Make sure that all newly planted trees and shrubs are well-watered. Do not let them dry out and pay particular care if there is a dry spell at this time of year.
- Sow seeds of vegetables such as peas, carrots and lettuces at fortnightly intervals so that you have a succession of young crops throughout the summer.
- Sow lettuce seeds in the same rows as parsnips. Parsnips take a long time to germinate and the lettuces will remind you where they have been sown. By the time the parsnips have germinated the lettuces will have been harvested and eaten.
- Make a chart of where you have sown the crops in your vegetable garden and make sure that you rotate the crops each season.
- Protect young plants from frost and birds with garden fleece. Birds are particularly partial to young peas.

- When weeding keep all perennial weeds separate and do not put them on your compost heap otherwise you will sow the next generation of weeds when you put the compost on your garden.
- Deadhead all daffodils and narcissi when they have finished flowering and feed the foliage with a foliar feed. Mark any clumps that appear to be overcrowded and split them up and replant them later on in the year.
- Apply selective weedkiller to perennial weeds such as nettles and thistles. Remember that many weeds can be eliminated by constant mowing or hoeing throughout the year, but don't, whatever you do, try to get rid of bindweed by anything other than chemical weedkiller. You will merely break the roots and thereby propagate more plants.

Viburnum × burkwoodii

sometimes damaged by rain or frost, but cherry blossom is one of the finest sights in a garden in spring. If you want to plant a cherry tree choose carefully to make sure you get one that will suit the space you give it and check with the nursery the likely height it will reach in five and ten years.

Rosmarinus
(Rosemary)
Rosemary, one of the most welcome plants in the herb garden, grows best against a sunny wall and has blue flowers early in the year. Two of the best varieties are *R. officinalis* 'Miss Jessopp's Upright' and *R. o.* Prostratus Group.

Ribes sanguineum

Prunus 'Taihaku'

Trillium

(Wood lily, Wake robin, Trinity flower)

Charming, rather short-lived, tuberous herbaceous perennials that prefer shady, moist, acid conditions. The flowers of *T. grandiflorum*, the most commonly grown variety, emerge pure white and then fade to a pale pink.

Viburnum x burkwoodii

Viburnums are amongst the best garden shrubs. They form a large genus and many of the shrubs have widely differing flowering periods and habits. *V. x burkwoodii* and its cultivars is evergreen and carries round clumps of white or pink flowers in spring. Like many viburnums it is heavily scented.

JOBS FOR THE MONTH

The greenhouse

- Sow seeds of outdoor tomatoes, runner beans, cucumbers, courgettes or marrows, and sweetcorn to plant out later in the year.
- Take dahlia cuttings and pot up pelargonium and fuchsia cuttings that you have taken earlier.
- Start begonia and gloxinia tubers into growth.
- Sow seeds of bedding plants and start to prick out or thin any seeds that you have sown earlier.
- Take leaf cuttings of common house plants, such as saintpaulias and streptocarpus.

Euphorbia characias ssp. *wulfenii*

29

LATE SPRING

By late spring as the days lengthen the garden year is in full swing. Daffodils give way to tulips and the delicate flowers of the aquilegia bring colour to the herbaceous border.

It is the time of the year for blossom, particularly apple blossom, possibly the loveliest of all with its delicate white and pink flowers. You need to look at it closely as it is often partially obscured by the young leaves that emerge at the same time. The other major gardening delights in late spring are the rhododendrons and azaleas, and if you are fortunate enough to live in the south-west or west of the country where they flower profusely, now is the time to visit the famous rhododendron gardens to see them in full bloom – great swathes of colour, so vivid that you can only stand and stare at the myriad flowers. Many rhododendrons are heavily scented, which adds to their attraction.

Apart from the garden the countryside looks its best at this time of the year. The leaves are young and green and have not yet acquired the heavy dusty look of high summer, the hedges are brightened by the hawthorn blossom and cow parsley and cowslips brings colour to the verges of the fields.

Gardens will need constant attention, particularly if you have a young garden that you are trying to establish. Keep a careful eye on the weather and if there is a dry spell make sure that all the new shrubs and trees that you have planted are well-watered. Seeds also need watching, watering and even protecting if a sudden and unexpected frost arrives – a most unwelcome visitor at this time of year. Weeds, alas, appear daily and if you can manage to control them now it will save a great deal of work later in the year. A walk round the garden each evening armed with rubber gloves and a small can of Roundup can pay huge dividends. Also watch out for the first signs of any pests and diseases, if you can spray them when they first appear, then they may be controlled for the rest of the year.

Kolkwitzia amabilis

THE FLOWERS AND SHRUBS OF ...

Ajuga reptans

Davidia involucrata

Ajuga
(Bugle)

A. reptans is one of the most decorative of the small ground-cover plants and spreads freely. It likes fertile moist soil and some shade. Among the most popular varieties are 'Atropurpurea', bronze-purple leaves, 'Braunherz', deep bronze leaves, 'Burgundy Glow', silvery-green leaves with red markings, and 'Catlin's Giant', large dark purple leaves. All ajugas have attractive erect spikes of blue flowers.

Aquilegia
(Columbine)

One of the favourite spring-flowering border plants, that has the merit (or demerit) of self-seeding freely. It requires little maintenance, it has delightful, delicate-looking flowers, ranging from deep purple, almost black, through pink and yellow to clear white and there are a number of hybrids and varieties available. The old cottage garden favourite *A. vulgaris*, Granny's bonnets, and its varieties, is still one of the best available.

Ceanothus
(Californian lilac)

Vigorous, usually evergreen, shrubs or small trees that can be so covered with blue flowers in late spring that the leaves may be totally hidden. There are autumn-flowering forms and white and pink varieties but most gardeners grow one of the spring-flowering varieties of which 'Blue Mound', 'Cascade' and 'Puget Blue' are among the best known. They are slightly tender and may require protection in hard winters, particularly when young.

Cercis
(Redbud)

The best-known species of this small genus is the Judas tree, *Cercis siliquastrum*, the tree from which Judas Iscariot is supposed to have hanged himself. It has pinkish-red flowers that appear on bare branches in spring. It flourishes best in a warm position in the garden.

Convallaria
(Lily-of-the-Valley)

A classic garden plant that may be difficult to establish. It likes shade and moist soil, and if the bulbs are happy with their lot they spread freely and produce sprays of deliciously scented white flowers in late spring. *C. majalis* var. *rosea* has pink flowers.

late

Convolvulus

(Bindweed)

The second-best known garden variety of this pernicious weed is *C. cneorum* that, rather surprisingly, turns out to be a compact shrub with silver leaves and attractive white flowers. It is not fully hardy and prefers full sun and dry, well-drained alkaline soil.

Cornus

(Dogwood)

A wonderful genus that includes many outstanding shrubs and small trees. Probably the most commonly grown is *C. alba* 'Sibirica' that has bright red bark in winter. The variety 'Elegantissima', also widely grown, has variegated leaves. Mature specimens of *C. kousa chinensis* and *C. alternifolia* 'Argentea' are among the most beautiful shrubs in the garden and are at their best is late spring. They prefer acid soil although some varieties will flourish in neutral conditions.

Crataegus

(Hawthorn)

Attractive small - to medium-sized trees that have bright red to white blossom in spring and bright red and yellow berries in the autumn when the leaves turn gold and scarlet. The most popular garden variety is probably *C. laevigata* 'Paul's Scarlet'.

Davidia involucrata

(Handkerchief tree)

So-called because of the large white bracts that surround the flowers in late spring and hang down from the branches. A bract is the technical term for a modified leaf that surrounds a flowerhead. These give the tree its ghostly appearance and another common name for it is the ghost tree.

33

spring LATE SPRING

JOBS FOR THE MONTH

The fruit and vegetable garden

- Put straw down in the strawberry bed, to protect the fruit from damp.
- Spray apple trees against pests after the blossom has set.
- Finish planting maincrop potatoes, earth up early potatoes, and protect them if frost threatens. Protect all the fruit and young vegetables from the attentions of birds.
- Plant out sweetcorn when the danger of frost has passed
- Sow seeds of brassicas: cabbage, cauliflowers, broccoli and Brussels sprouts.
- Make a trellis of bamboo canes and plant out runner beans raised indoors or plant two seeds at the foot of each cane. Discard one if both seeds germinate.
- Plant out any brassicas that you have raised from seed.
- Start thinning carrots, spinach and lettuces and sow seeds of beetroot.
- Sow more carrots and lettuce and sow French beans.
- If you want a herb garden prepare and plant one now.
- At the end of the month plant out courgettes and marrows on a pile of garden compost.
- To keep the weeds down in the kitchen garden lay two or three sheets of newspaper down when you plant brassicas, cut holes in the paper, plant through the holes and then cover the paper with garden compost.
- If you want to grow mint, plant it in an old bucket. This will stop it spreading.

Dicentra

(Bleeding heart, Dutchman's trousers) A favourite garden perennial that flowers early in the year. *D. spectabilis*, pink and white flowers, and *D. s. f. alba*, white flowers, are the two large varieties most generally found but *D. formosa* and *D.* 'Stuart Boothman' are much smaller with attractive grey-green foliage and charming pink flowers reminiscent of stalks of heather. They spread freely.

Erysimum

(Wallflower) These now include those plants previously called cheiranthus. They are normally grown as biennials, flowering the year after they have been planted out, *E. cheiri* Bedder Series is particularly popular. The yellow, orange and red flowers of all wallflowers are beautifully scented.

Exochorda

(Pearl bush) Another favourite late-spring flowering shrub. The most popular variety is *E. × macrantha* 'The Bride' that forms a dense mound covered with long racemes of white flowers.

Geranium

(Cranesbill) Not to be confused with pelargoniums, geraniums are a large genus of hardy perennials that no garden should be

Exochorda racemosa

without. There are a number of outstanding varieties that flower throughout the summer; among the most popular are *G.* 'Johnson's Blue', violet-blue flowers, *G. × oxonianum* 'Claridge Druce' and *G. endressii*, pink flowers and *G. clarkei* 'Kashmir White', white flowers.

Iris

There are a number of different irises and many flower at different times of the year. The most popular garden iris is the bearded iris that flowers in late spring: there are many varieties in varied colours of white, yellow and purple. The common iris, *I. pseudacorus*, the common flag, is usually found growing in water-logged soil beside ponds.

Potentilla fruticosa 'Primrose Beauty'

Kolkwitzia amabilis
(Beauty bush)
A compact shrub grown for its profusion of pink flowers that emerge in late spring. The variety 'Pink Cloud' has slightly deeper pink flowers.

Laburnum
(Golden rain)
Well-known trees with long yellow racemes of pea-like yellow flowers, they make good specimen trees in a small garden or can be grown as an avenue. Beware if you have children, the seeds and flowers of laburnum are highly poisonous.

Myosotis
(Forget-me-not)
The forget-me-not may be a humble plant, but it is brilliantly invasive and can be used with great effect to carpet a rose bed with its blue flowers or fill in a corner in a herbaceous border. The alpine forms, *M. alpestris*, are the most compact.

Osteospermum
Popular garden sub-shrubs and perennials that are grown for their daisy-like flowers. They are not fully hardy and in the colder parts of the country are best grown as annuals. The varieties come in a number of colours: yellow, white, purple and pink. 'Whirligig' has the most extraordinary shaped flowerhead.

Potentilla
(Cinquefoil)
A varied genus of plants, the best-known is the shrubby potentilla, *P. fruticosa* and its varieties that is grown in a mixed shrub border or sometimes as an informal hedge.

Geranium sanguineum var. *striatum*

The flower and shrub garden

- Treat the lawn with selective weedkiller and fertiliser if necessary.
- Clear spring flower beds if you have them.
- When the primulas have finished flowering dig up the clumps, then split them and replant them with a scattering of bonemeal to make more plants.
- Deadhead tulip bulbs after flowering, then lift them and heel them in to the kitchen garden to let the foliage die back naturally. After that, dig up and store the bulbs until the time comes to plant them out in the autumn. Make sure that you label them correctly for one tulip bulb looks much like another when it doesn't have flowers attached. This advice also applies to dahlia tubers that are lifted and stored over winter.
- Prune early-flowering shrubs, if necessary, after flowering.
- Feed roses and spray if signs of greenfly, black spot or mildew appear.
- Start taking softwood cuttings of those shrubs that can be propagated in this way.
- If you garden on alkaline soil and are trying to grow lime-hating plants, water them all with chelated iron or flowers of sulphur to raise the acidity of the soil and mulch them with peat.

- As the weather becomes warmer and the danger of late frosts passes you can plant out half-hardy annuals, and sow seeds of hardy annuals, such as godetia, nigella (love-in-a-mist), clarkia and candytuft.
- This is also the time to sow seeds of hardy biennials such as wallflowers, Sweet Williams and Canterbury bells, as well as hardy perennials, such as hollyhocks, lupins and delphiniums. This is easy to do and you can save a good deal of money, provided you are prepared to wait for a year before the plants flower. Seed is considerably cheaper than plants purchased from a garden centre or nursery.
- Finish planting out gladioli and summer bulbs.
- Plant out dahlia tubers.
- Sow seeds of rock garden plants if you have a rockery to which you want to add a selection of plants.
- At the end of the month, when all danger of late frosts has passed, plant out summer bedding plants and plant up window boxes, containers and hanging baskets.
- Watch the gardeners in the local parks and do not plant out any summer bedding until you see that they are doing the same. This is a very good guide to avoid damage from late frosts.

Primula denticulata

Primula
(Primrose)

A large complicated genus with many different types that can be divided into a number of botanical sections. In spite of this the common primrose, *P. vulgaris*, that can be found growing wild in many parts of the country, remains a firm favourite with its pale-yellow, slightly scented flowers.

Rhododendrons

The largest genus of plants with well over 500 species now includes those plants formerly classified separately as azaleas. Many rhododendrons are evergreen and a number have heavily scented flowers. They will really only grow well in moist, warm, acid soil and partial shade, and are best seen in the gardens of Cornwall and the West Country in spring. Small azaleas can be grown in town gardens and can make good plants for tubs on patios in shade providing they are not allowed to dry out.

Skimmia japonica 'Tansley Gem'

Skimmia japonica

A useful small evergreen shrub that flourishes in the border and grows well in town gardens as they prefer at least partial shade. Depending on the variety you may need to grow both male and female plants for them to bear fruit.

Tulipa

(Tulip)

There are a lot of tulips and no space in a book of this nature even to describe the various groups of which there are fifteen. Tulips are usually grown in borders and care should be taken to group the types and colour carefully so that they flower at the same time. They look lovely grown in a bed with forget-me-nots.

Viburnum plicatum

(Japanese snowball bush)

Another outstanding garden shrub with white flowers, and leaves that turn bright red in autumn.

V. p. 'Grandiflorum' has large white flowers and *V. p.* 'Mariesii' has layered branches along which large white flowers appear in spring, as if they were being held out for admiration.

Tulipa 'Menton'

JOBS FOR THE MONTH

The greenhouse

- Plant greenhouse tomatoes in growbags and plant peppers, cucumbers and aubergines if you plan to grow them.
- Feed potted plants and seedlings regularly.
- Prick out any late-sown bedding plants.
- If you have a greenhouse vine prune it and thin out the grapes if you have too many bunches.
- Gradually stop watering bulbs of amaryllis and *Cyclamen persicum*, the indoor cyclamen, as the leaves die down.

Summer

EARLY SUMMER

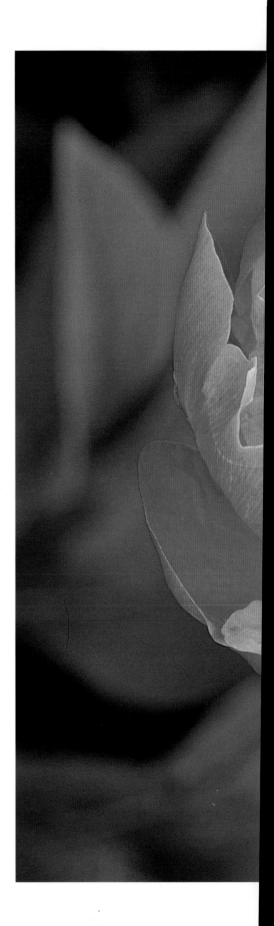

Many gardens look their best in early summer. The tulips and forget-me-nots of late spring die away and are succeeded by the blossom of the crab apple trees, and the dangling tresses of flowers on the wisteria vines. Colour returns to the herbaceous border, flowers appear on the first of the hardy geraniums, the bearded flag irises bloom, peonies, poppies and lupins start to flower and everywhere buds start to turn to blossom. As midsummer approaches the scent of the philadelphus fills the air in the evening, while many of the rhododendrons are still in full flower.

This is the month when the first flush of roses appears, brightening gardens throughout the land. It is a season of vigorous growth; trees, shrubs and plants make more rapid progress now than at any other time of the year and the gardener should take advantage by sowing seeds, planting out all the plants that are tender and taking cuttings to increase the stock of herbaceous favourites, such as catmint and pinks.

When all danger of late frosts has finally passed the gardener can plant out tender summer bedding plants as well as vegetables, such as courgettes, marrows, tomatoes and sweetcorn, raised indoors or under glass.

As always it is important to keep an eye on the weather. If a sudden frost returns or is threatened, many young plants can be protected by a temporary covering of garden fleece, young growth is much more susceptible to frost damage than mature trees and shrubs. Also if there is a very dry spell, keep all newly planted trees and shrubs well-watered. All young shrubs take some time to become established and their growth can be retarded if they are starved of water in their first year or two of life.

Paeonia lactiflora 'Bowl of Beauty'

THE FLOWERS AND SHRUBS OF ...

Anthemis

A popular genus of perennials with daisy-like flowers that bloom in early summer and continue for many weeks. Two good choices are; *A. punctata* ssp. *cupaniana*, white flowers with yellow centres, and *A. tinctoria*, the golden marguerite or ox-eye chamomile and its varieties, that has yellow flowers.

Argyranthemum

A genus of evergreen sub-shrubs that are covered with daisy-like flowers for many weeks in summer. 'Jamaica Primrose' has single yellow flowers and 'Vancouver' has double anemone-centred pink flowers.

Artemisia

(Sagebrush, Wormwood)

A large genus with over 300 species, many artemisias are grown for their beautiful silver foliage only. The flowerheads, rather small and an insignificant yellow in colour, are removed before the flowers develop. Among the most popular varieties are *A. ludoviciana* var. *latiloba* , *A. l.* 'Silver Queen' and *A.* 'Powis Castle'.

Centranthus ruber

(Valerian)

A hardy standby for the herbaceous border that spreads freely and may require control. The flowers are various shades of pink to red. *C. r. albus* has white flowers and is less vigorous.

Cistus

(Rock rose)

Small shrubs that come from the south of Europe and need full sun and a warm place in the garden. They have showy flowers and among the best-known is *C. x cyprius* that has crinkled white petals with showy red spots at the base and yellow stamens.

Corydalis

(Fumitory)

Attractive, vigorous, ground-cover perennial with delicate fern-like, green leaves and long tubular flowers that last for several weeks. The best varieties are *C. flexuosa*, blue flowers, *C. lutea*, yellow, and *C. solida*, red to pink. They spread freely.

Crambe cordifolia

(Giant sea kale)

A spectacular large garden perennial that can only be grown in a big border. It carries a mass of small white flowers above giant dark green leaves that have the sweetest honey scent that fills the air.

Eremurus

(Foxtail lily, King's spear)

Another spectacular garden perennial with long single spikes of flowers. They flower best in a sheltered position and prefer slightly acid soil. *E. himalaicus* bears white flowers and *E. robustus*, pink

Gunnera

(Prickly rhubarb)

Clump-forming herbaceous perennials, the most commonly grown is the giant *G. manicata* that develops vast leaves and has spikes of reddish flowers in midsummer. It is grown in boggy soil beside ponds or waterways.

Helianthemum

(Sun rose)

Small sun-loving sub-shrubs that flower from late spring onwards and are ideal plants for the rock garden or sunny south-facing beds. Many have attractive grey-green leaves. 'Fire

42

JOBS FOR THE MONTH

The fruit and vegetable garden

- Thin the seeds that you have sown earlier. This applies to carrots, beetroot, parsnips, turnips and lettuces.
- Plant out winter vegetables such as leeks, greens and celery.
- Pick the first peas.

early

Lilum 'Connecticut King'

Dragon' (vivid orange), 'Rhodanthe Carneum' (delicate pale pink) and 'Wisley Primrose' (pale yellow) are among the best varieties.

Lilium

(Lily)

A large genus of graceful plants that can be found in flower from late spring to autumn. There are nine divisions according to parentage and country of origin. Lilies are generally grown from bulbs, and among the most popular are *L. candidum*, the Madonna lily, *L. martagon*, the common Turk's cap lily, with its pinkish flowers, and *L. regale*, the Regal lily, which is strongly scented. All lilies will require staking.

Paeonia

(Peony, peony rose)

Peonies are excellent plants for the mixed border and are often long-lived, but they resent being moved and can take time to become established. There are two forms: the garden perennial and the upright deciduous shrub, the tree peony. The flowers, often double or semi-double, are generally red, pink or white although there are yellow varieties. The most attractively named peony is *P. mlokosewitschii*, popularly called Molly-the-Witch, that has single

yellow flowers. *P. suffruticosa* and its varieties is the best-known tree peony and has spectacular flowers, sometimes as large as 25 cm (10 in) across.

Papaver

(Poppy)

Poppies are either loved or hated in the garden. Some gardeners pull them out whenever they find them, others welcome them as easy, self-seeding plants that require little effort. The best poppies for the garden are *P. orientale*, the Oriental

43

EARLY SUMMER

JOBS FOR THE MONTH

The flower and shrub garden

- At this time of the year it is important to keep on top of the routine tasks, such as weeding and grass cutting. Weeds flourish, especially if there is any amount of rain, and they are best controlled by selective weedkiller or constant hoeing. The old garden saying 'One year's seeds is seven years weeds' has a certain amount of truth in it.
- Prune shrubs that require it when they have finished flowering.
- Cut back pyracantha and chaenomeles to keep them in shape, particularly if they are grown against a wall, to encourage the formation of flowering and fruiting spurs.
- Spray roses.
- Pull off any suckers of roses, lilac and plum trees.
- If you grow rhododendrons and want to increase your stock, layer the plants now; propagate clematis by layering.
- Cut back any spent flowers in the rock garden and take cuttings of any plants where you want to increase your stock.
- Cut back hardy geraniums when they have flowered for the first time. This will encourage them to flower again.
- Plant out summer bedding plants if you have not done this earlier.
- Sow seeds of hardy biennials if you have not done this the previous month.
- Deadhead all plants regularly as this encourages further flowers.
- Water plants if there is a prolonged dry spell. Give the plants a really good soak once a week.

poppy, that bears large crumpled cup-shaped flowers in colours from orange, white pink or red – most flowers are strongly marked in the centre. *P. somniferum,* the Opium poppy, has large seed heads and double flowers.

Philadelphus
(Mock orange)
A deciduous shrub grown for its attractive white flowers, sometimes with marked centres, that have a wonderful, overpowering scent in summer. The various species and varieties have a number of differing growth habits so take care that you purchase one that suits the size of your garden. Among the best are: 'Belle Etoile', *delavayi,* 'Manteau d'Hermine' and 'Virginal', the last variety is very vigorous and can reach 3 m (10 ft) or more.

Robinia
Two species of the genus are found in some gardens: *R. pseudoacacia,* the False acacia tree, has dark green leaves and long racemes of white flowers in early summer, the variety *R. p.* 'Frisia' has yellow leaves; and *R. hispida,* the rose acacia, a deciduous shrub with long racemes of pink flowers in early summer.

Santolina
(Cotton lavender)
A useful sub-shrub that flourishes on light soil in full sun. *S. chamaecyparissus*

Syringa vulgaris 'Vestale'

has grey-green leaves, the variety 'Lambrook Silver' has silver leaves. They are best cut back fairly hard after flowering.

Stachys
(Betony)
One of the best ground-cover plants in the garden. This is quite a large genus but few are worth cultivating: the best-known are *S. byzantina,* Lamb's ears or Loppylugs, that has intensely silver-white, felted leaves and small pink flowers in summer and *S. b.* 'Silver Carpet' with silver leaves. This variety does not flower and is grown entirely for its foliage.

Syringa
(Lilac)
There are a number of species but the most commonly grown is *S. vulgaris* and its varieties. These flower from late spring to early summer in shades of lilac, purple, pink

and white, and the flowers are often deliciously scented. They are difficult to control for, if pruned hard, they will not flower the following year.

Tiarella cordifolia

(Foam flower)
A useful ground-cover plant that carries a profusion of white flowers on upright spikes in summer. They need moist shade to flourish and the leaves often turn brilliant red or orange in the autumn.

Weigela

Attractive shrubs that are grown for their normally pinkish-red flowers in early summer, although some varieties have white or yellow flowers. They have a somewhat straggly habit and should be pruned after flowering.

Wisteria

One of the most popular climbers that carries lovely pendant tresses (racemes) of fragrant white or lilac flowers in early summer. The varieties generally found in gardens are *W. sinensis*, the Chinese wisteria, and *W. floribunda*, the Japanese wisteria. They need very careful pruning if they are to flower properly, but even when pruned correctly, twice a year, in early spring and late summer, a new plant may not flower for a number of years.

45

Wisteria

JOBS FOR THE MONTH

The greenhouse

- Feed potted plants regularly and remember to water them.
- Feed indoor tomatoes when the first truss of fruit has set and continue to feed them every fortnight or so.
- Pot up and pot on all seedlings as necessary.

ROSES

Roses can be divided into numerous categories and anyone wanting to learn something about the history and types of roses available is advised to get the catalogue of one of the many reputable rose specialists.

In an attempt to simplify the categories I have divided roses into three main divisions: bush roses, climbers and ramblers and shrub roses. Bush roses include the hybrid tea and floribunda (many-flowered) roses that can be found in most gardens throughout the country, as well as patio and miniature roses. Climbers and ramblers are the roses that climb up walls and through trees. Ramblers are more vigorous than climbers – there are a number of lovely, fairly small, modern climbers very suitable for small town gardens. The last main category is shrub roses, roses that form a shrub when mature. These include the old-fashioned roses that are correctly divided into a number of different groups such as gallicas, albas, damasks and moss roses, and the lovely modern English roses bred by David Austin.

R. Iceberg

'Albéric Barbier'
(rambler)
A rambler rose that can grow to 8 m (25 ft) within three years. It has yellow buds that open to double creamy-white flowers. It is very vigorous and will quickly cover a wall, and the glossy, green foliage lasts a long time during the winter.

'Albertine'
(rambler)
A favourite rose, although not as vigorous as 'Albéric Barbier', its only fault is that it only flowers once in midsummer. The buds are deep pink while the flowers are paler and the flowers give off the most wonderful, unmistakable scent. It needs to be pruned after flowering.

'Ballerina'
(shrub)
A fairly modern polyantha shrub rose that carries a profusion of pale pink, single flowers with white centres. They are much the same colour as apple blossom. It is most reliable, flowers all summer and has a slight scent.

'Félicité Perpétue'
(rambler)
One of the best rambler roses that can reach 6 m (19 ft). From midsummer onwards it has a mass of small pompom-shaped, creamy-white flowers that are edged with pink, and have a delicate fragrance.

Fragrant Cloud
(bush, hybrid tea)
Large, shapely, dark red flowers with a strong fragrance and dark green leaves. It will reach 1 m (3 ft).

R. Peace

Golden Showers
(modern climber)
One of the most popular modern climbing roses that has large, double, deep yellow blooms and flowers freely throughout the summer. The flowers are fragrant. Rather surprisingly, given its colour, it will grow on a north-facing wall and reaches 3 m (10 ft).

Graham Thomas
(shrub)
A lovely shrub rose named after one of the most influential gardeners of the 20th century. It has clear, rich, yellow, cupped flowers with strong fragrance and shiny pale green leaves.
1.2 m × 1.2 m (4 ft × 4 ft).

46

R. xanthina 'Canary Bird'

Iceberg
(bush, floribunda)
One of the most popular roses with shapely white flowers that become tinged with pink later in the year. It flowers continuously from summer onwards and makes a shrub 1.2 m (4 ft) high. Climbing Iceberg is the graceful climbing form.

'Louise Odier'
(shrub, Bourbon)
A strong, bushy, old-fashioned rose bred in 1851 with large, perfectly formed, cupped pink flowers that are strongly fragrant. It flowers continuously throughout the summer. 1.5 × 1.2 m (5 ft × 4 ft).

'Mme Alfred Carrière'
(climber)
An old rose (noisette) that has been a popular climber for years. It has white fragrant double flowers that are tinted pink. It will reach 6 m (20 ft).

'Maigold'
(climber)
This rose has lovely, fragrant, bronze-yellow, semi-double flowers but only really flowers once in the summer. However it is very disease-resistant, tolerates poor conditions and is one of the roses that can be grown on a north wall. It will reach 4 m (13 ft).

'New Dawn'
(modern climber)
A deservedly popular climbing rose bred in 1930. It has shapely silvery-pink, fragrant flowers that continue through the summer and it will tolerate a shady site. It will reach 3 m (10 ft).

Peace
(bush, hybrid tea)
Eternally popular rose with lovely yellow-pink flowers. Appropriately it was bred in 1945 and flowers reliably throughout the summer.

Rosa rugosa
(shrub)
A wild rose that repeat flowers and is sometimes grown as a hedge. The flowers are single, purple-red in colour and it has large hips. Tolerates poor conditions and will reach 2 m × 2 m (7 ft × 7 ft).

'Zéphirine Drouhin'
(climber, Bourbon)
The thornless rose that is very popular with many on account of this. It also grows well on a north wall and carries a continuous succession of fragrant reddish-pink flowers throughout the summer. 4 m (13 ft).

R. 'Louise Odier'

47

MIDSUMMER

In midsummer the garden reaches its full beauty. Even though most of the flowering trees and shrubs are now past their best, the flower beds and borders are ablaze with colour as the flowers of summer come into full bloom. Lavender bushes produce their first sprigs of blue and they and the summer lilies make the air heavy with scent.

Bedding plants are now at their best and the bright red pelargoniums and white and blue petunias and lobelia brighten many a border and hanging basket. Some gardeners also grow tobacco plants, nicotiana, just for the smell that they give off every evening; another flower at its best now, is the evening primrose, which opens its pale yellow flowers as the heat goes out of the day.

However, for all the colour available, it is a time of the year when gardens can look a little tired. The true gardening enthusiast can plant a number of perennials that flower rather later in the summer, and these help to keep the borders bright and fresh for the next two months.

In many ways the gardener's year now starts to wind down. The long summer evenings give the gardener the chance to get the garden in order; growth is no longer so exuberant and everyone can relax, sit and enjoy the summer sun. It is the time of the year when the large-flowered clematis festoon the walls of cottages and scramble up pergolas and over arches. These flowers, more than any other, typify the true cottage garden at the height of summer.

Midsummer also brings the first vegetables of the year to the table. You can look forward to harvesting the early peas, the sugarsnap varieties (mangetout), where both pod and peas are eaten, are particularly delicious, and the first early potatoes and broad beans make vegetable dishes fit for a god. Early lettuce, too, will now be ready and the first plums will be ripening on the trees.

Clematis 'Jackmanii'

48

THE FLOWERS AND SHRUBS OF ...

JOBS FOR THE MONTH

The fruit and vegetable garden

- Summer prune any fruit trees you are growing as espaliers or cordons.
- Cut back the laterals on gooseberry bushes to make the fruit easier to pick.
- Sow seeds of spring cabbage and continue to sow carrots and lettuces in succession.
- Make sure that the plants in the vegetable garden have sufficient water.
- Pinch out the tops of tomato plants when they have set five trusses of fruit and pinch out all the side shoots.
- Harvest some of the early potatoes and lift shallots when the leaves have turned yellow. Store them in a cool dry place.
- Turn over the compost heap. This helps decomposition.
- Pick and eat strawberries and raspberries and any other berries that you grow.

Hosta fortunei var. albopicta

Acanthus
(Bear's breeches)
Popular herbaceous perennials grown mainly for their architectural interest. The most common species found in gardens is *A. spinosus* that has tall plumes of white flowers covered by purple bracts in midsummer.

Achillea
(Yarrow)
Another useful garden perennial, *A. filipendulina* 'Gold Plate' is grown in many gardens and has large flat heads of yellow flowers. It is a useful plant for the back of a border. *A. ptarmica*, sneezewort, and its varieties has white flowers, others are pink.

Alchemilla
(Lady's mantle)
A large genus of plants, the most commonly grown form is *A. mollis*, a plant that provokes strong reactions from many gardeners. It is very vigorous and invasive and while some love its soft green foliage and delicate yellow flowers, others have been known to spray it with weedkiller to remove it from their borders.

Astilbe
Clump-forming perennials with long spires of generally red or pink flowers held upright above the leaves.

A. 'Brautschleier' is white, 'Bressingham Beauty' is pink. They like moist conditions and full sun.

Buddleja
(Butterfly bush)
So-called because the flowers attract both bees and butterflies, the plant is named after the Rev. Adam Buddle, a vicar from Essex. The best known buddleja is *B. davidii* and its varieties, that carries long sprays of flowers in varying colours from deep blue to purple, red and white. *B. davidii* flowers on the new wood produced in the current year and needs to be cut back hard early in the spring.

Campanula
(Bellflower)
A large genus of annuals, biennials and perennials that vary in size from *C. carpatica*, one of the most attractive ground-cover perennials, to *C. lactiflora*, the milky bellflower, that can reach a height of 1.5 m (5 ft). Campanulas usually come in shades of blue or purple with some white varieties.

Clematis
Late-flowering clematis (Group 3) start to flower from midsummer onwards. The most spectacular of these climbing plants are the large-

mid

flowered varieties, such as 'Jackmanii', deep purple, 'Comtesse de Bouchaud', pink, and 'Mme Edouard André', red with yellow anthers.

Delphinium

Delphiniums are one of the best-loved flowers of summer and add height and colour to any herbaceous border. Delphiniums, traditionally, are blue, but they are available in a range of colours from white, pink, orange and yellow. All need staking and are best propagated by basal cuttings in early spring.

Geranium

Varieties of *G. pratense*, the Meadow cranesbill, flower from midsummer onwards, followed by *G. wallichianum*.

Hosta

(Plantain lily)
Clump-forming perennials that are grown entirely for their spectacular, coloured leaves, from cream and yellow to smoky blue, although they do also have attractive small spikes of white or violet flowers in midsummer. They are, however, particularly loved by slugs and snails and the gardener must be vigilant if he or she is to preserve hostas from these pests.

Hypericum

(St John's wort)
A large genus of plants that includes *H. calycinum,* the Rose of Sharon. They all have yellow flowers and many have foliage that turns reddish orange in autumn. The most commonly grown is *H.* 'Hidcote', a semi-evergreen shrub, often grown as a low informal hedge.

Jasminum officinale

(Common jasmine)
A well-known twining climber with fragrant white flowers that will climb

summer

MIDSUMMER

JOBS FOR THE MONTH

The flower and shrub garden

- Watch out for weeds throughout the garden and keep on top of them with the hoe or weedkiller spray.
- Deadhead roses and other flowers regularly. This particularly applies to annuals, such as petunias and pelargoniums.
- Prune rambling roses when their flowering season is over. Some, such as 'Albertine' and 'Chaplin's Pink', can present quite a pruning problem and it is a good thing to consult a specialist manual for precise instructions.
- Do not cut the lawn too short, especially if there is a prolonged spell of dry weather.
- Take softwood and semi-ripe cuttings of any shrubs that you wish to propagate. Prepare a special cutting bed in the kitchen garden or a cold frame that you use for this purpose.
- Water and feed pot plants regularly.
- Clip deciduous hedges and also yew and conifer hedges.
- Plant bulbs of autumn-flowering crocus, colchicum, hardy cyclamen and *Amaryllis belladonna*.

over any suitable support. It is semi-evergreen in mild areas and unless you have an infinity of space available it will need to be strictly controlled as it is very vigorous. It is best to thin out the shoots and cut back when flowering is over.

Lathyrus
(Everlasting pea)
A large genus that contains over 150 species, although gardeners usually concentrate on just three or four. The most important is *L. odoratus*, the sweet pea, that is grown usually in kitchen gardens up a framework of bamboos for cutting for the house. Many colourful varieties have been developed and the flowers have a delicious fresh scent. *L. grandiflorus* and *L. latifolius*, the everlasting pea, are both climbing perennials with pink to purple flowers and are best grown up pillars in borders.

Lavandula
(Lavender)
Very aromatic evergreen small shrubs or sub-shrubs that are grown as low hedges along borders or in beds. The best-known varieties are *L. angustifolia* 'Hidcote', deep purple flowers, *L. x intermedia*, English lavender, light blue to violet flowers, and *L. stoechas*, French lavender, that has purple flowers and showy purple bracts.

Lysimachia nummularia

Lonicera
(Honeysuckle)
Honeysuckles are a large genus grown for their flowers and scent and are extremely popular plants in cottage gardens. Early climbing honeysuckles, varieties of *L. japonica*, flower from late spring onwards, 'Halliana' is the best known, with flowers that open white and turn to darker yellow with age. *L. periclymenum* 'Belgica', early Dutch honeysuckle, has white and yellow flowers, streaked with red, and *L. p.* 'Serotina', late Dutch honeysuckle, carries creamy-white flowers, reddish-purple on the outside. Both flower from midsummer onwards.

Lonicera periclymenum 'Belgica'

Lupinus
(Lupins)
Herbaceous border favourites that have been popular plants for many years. The majority of the lupins grown are Russell Hybrids that form substantial clumps and carry large spikes of flowers in many colours. Lupins are somewhat prone to pests and disease and are best renewed every four years or so. They are poisonous and should be avoided if small children use the garden.

Lysimachia
(Loosestrife)
Perhaps better known as a wildflower the genus contains two well-known garden perennials: *L. clethroides*, a spreading perennial that has long spikes of white flowers in summer, and *L. nummularia*, creeping Jenny, that is often grown as a ground-cover plant in wild areas of the garden.

Oenothera
(Evening primrose)
There is a number of species grown in gardens. The true evening primrose *O. biennis* reaches a height of 1–1.5 m (3–5 ft) and has the most beautiful pale yellow, fragrant, cup-shaped flowers that darken as they get older. It flowers throughout the summer. Other species commonly found are

O. macrocarpa syn. *O. missouriensis* and *O. perennis* that are lower growing. Many evening primroses have a creeping habit.

Penstemon
A deservedly popular genus of evergreen, or semi-evergreen, garden perennials grown for their long spikes of tubular, bell-shaped flowers in colours ranging from deep red through to pale pink and white. Among the most attractive are *P.* 'Andenken an Friedrich Hahn' , that used to be known, more descriptively, as 'Garnet', deep red flowers, 'Apple Blossom', pink and white, and 'White Bedder', white that becomes tinged with pink as it ages.

Tradescantia
(Spiderwort, Flower-of-a-day)
An attractive, no-problem plant for the herbaceous border that commemorates John Tradescant, gardener to Charles I. The best and most commonly grown varieties, are the andersoniana hybrids that have flowers in colours ranging from the deepest purple through blue to white.

Lupins 'Russell Hybrids'

53

JOBS FOR THE MONTH

The greenhouse
- Pot on any seeds sown in the spring.
- Feed potted plants.
- Pinch out the growing tip of aubergines and allow only one fruit per shoot.
- Watch out for any pests and diseases and spray as appropriate when they appear.

ANNUALS AND BIENNIALS

Annuals and biennials are a blessing for the gardener who wants plenty of bright colour in the garden during the summer but has little time to spend. Hardy annuals can be sown directly into the ground where they are to flower and half-hardy annuals and biennials can be bought from nurseries and garden centres as young plants and then planted out when the weather is good and the timing convenient. Generally annuals prefer a sunny position and they flower all summer long providing an endless succession of colour that is only ended by the first frosts of the autumn.

Ageratum
Half-hardy annuals with small powder-puff shaped flowerheads usually in varying shades of blue although pink and white varieties are available. The dwarf varieties are the ones most commonly grown.

annuals

Antirrhinum
(Snapdragon)
These are short-lived perennials that are usually treated as half-hardy annuals. They have stiff spikes of flowers with a pronounced lip and come in many colours from yellow, pink, red and bronze to white. The Tahiti series are smaller than many other varieties and are disease resistant.

Begonia x carrieri syn. B. semperflorens
The fibrous-rooted begonias flower from early summer until the first frosts of winter. They are usually found in shades of pink, red or white and have reddish-bronze leaves.

Bellis perennis
(Daisy)
A spring-flowering perennial usually grown as an annual. It has showy pompon-like flowers and is available in a number of series with different shaped flowerheads and colours.

Calendula officinalis
(Pot marigold)
A cottage garden plant with an easily recognisable orange and yellow flower. The Pacific series has double flowers in varying shades of orange and cream with some bicoloured varieties.

Cosmos bipinnatus
Elegant, daisy-like, flowers that bloom in the second half of the summer in shades of red, pink and white. The variety 'Sensation Mixed' is popular with mixed colours.

Dianthus barbatus
(Sweet William)
Another cottage garden favourite that has broad heads of sweet scented flowers, usually in shades of red, pink and white. Some varieties have bronze or tinted leaves.

Eschscholzia californica
(Californian poppy)
An easy-to-grow annual that carries poppy-shaped flowers usually yellow or orange, although some pink and white varieties are available. 'Ballerina' has semi-double flowers.

Iberis umbellata
(Common candytuft)
Candytuft has dense clusters of small flowers in varying shades from white through to pink, red and purple. A number of varieties are available.

Top Left:
Ageratum houstonianum
'Blue Danube'

Top Right:
Antirrhinum

Bottom Left:
Begonia semperflorens

Bottom Right:
Bellis perennis

55

ANNUALS AND BIENNIALS

Impatiens

(Busy Lizzie)
Deservedly popular plants that are ideal for containers and hanging baskets that flower throughout the summer. The New Guinea hybrids have larger flowers and variegated or bronze foliage.

Lavatera

(Mallow)
Commonly grown as a hardy annual lavatera has the distinctive five-petalled mallow flowers and soft, deep green, hairy leaves. A number of varieties are available in shades of red, white and pink.

Nemesia

A dainty, erect, half-hardy annual that bears its flowers on the end of spikes. These are available in many colours ranging from pink, blue, purple, red and white, some varieties are bi-coloured.

Top Left: *Dianthus barbatus* Harbinger Mixed
Middle Left: *Eschscholzia califomica*
Bottom Left: *Calendula officinalis*
Top Right: *Erysimum* x *allionii*
Middle Right: *Iberis umbellata* 'Fairyland'
Bottom Right: *Cosmos* Sensation Mixed

Nigella damascena
(Love-in-a-mist)
Usually available in deep violet or white this popular annual self-seeds freely and is valuable as a cut or dried flower.

Petunia
Probably the most popular annual of all, available in a wide variety of colours. The Super Cascade Series is especially good for planting in hanging baskets.

Pulsatilla vulgaris
(Pasque flower)
A clump-forming perennial often grown as a bedding plant, it has bell-shaped purple flowers in spring.

Tagetes
(African marigold)
Half-hardy annuals usually found in shades of yellow and orange. They are particularly useful grown in the vegetable garden for the smell they give off deters cabbage white butterflies from laying their eggs on the brassicas.

Top Left: *Impatiens walleriana*
Middle Left: *Petunia* 'Vogue'
Bottom Left: *Nemesia* 'Carnival'
Top Right: *Lavatera* 'Parade'
Middle Right: *Tagetes* 'Lemon Gem'
Bottom Right: Regal pelargonium

LATE SUMMER

This is the month for holidays, a time when even the keenest gardener can contemplate a week or a fortnight away from home without the possibility of the garden being overtaken by too many disasters in his or her absence. There is still plenty of colour about, summer bedding plants are still in full bloom, particularly if they are deadheaded regularly: antirrhinums, verbena and ageratum are some of the favourite plants that give good colour at this time of the year, while in the borders the hollyhocks stand tall and colourful, surrounded by the phlox and summer bulbs, such as galtonia and agapanthus, and in the rose garden the second flush of flowers will give blooms and colours to rival the first flush of the year. In the rock garden it is the time of year for the lovely *Gentiana sino-ornata*, with its beautiful blue flowers, that emerges at the same time as the delicate edelweiss. The robust hypericum, St John's wort, is another favourite garden plant that flowers at its best in this month.

In the kitchen garden many of the choice berries are now over, but the early apples are now ready and can be picked and eaten. They will not keep and should be enjoyed as they ripen, so if you realise too large a crop, give them away. In the vegetable garden more and more vegetables are now ready – carrots and small turnips, peas and the first French beans, to be followed by courgettes. There is a great satisfaction to be had from growing vegetables, so ignore the scoffers, who say that they are available more cheaply from the shelves of the local supermarket, the ones you grow and harvest yourself taste far, far better.

Osteospermum 'Buttermilk'

THE FLOWERS AND SHRUBS OF ...

JOBS FOR THE MONTH

The fruit and vegetable garden

- Make a new strawberry bed, planting out runners from your old plants, unless you wish to order a new variety.
- Prune blackcurrant bushes when fruiting is over.
- Watch out for attack by caterpillars on all brassicas. They can wipe out a crop almost overnight. Butterflies can be deterred from laying their eggs on brassicas by planting deterrent crops such as tagetes, African marigolds, or tomatoes, or by covering the plants with a fine-meshed garden net.
- Start picking early apples as they ripen.
- Pick currants and raspberries and cut down the old raspberry canes when they have finished fruiting.
- Lift and store onions as they ripen. Lift them in a dry period and allow them to dry off outside before plaiting them into onion strings.
- Pick all the vegetables that you require and prepare and freeze crops such as peas where you cannot eat all the crop at once.

Begonia

A large genus of annuals, perennials, shrubs and climbers, the main begonias found in this country are the tuberous and semperflorens varieties grown as bedding plants in summer gardens: they have spectacular, colourful flowers. Tuberous begonias are lifted in autumn and overwintered in a frost-free greenhouse and then started into growth in the spring. Semperflorens begonias are evergreen perennials usually grown in containers that are brought indoors during the winter.

Caryopteris

A genus of scented deciduous shrubs with silvery-grey leaves and blue flowers born on the current year's growth. They make attractive plants in a mixed border.

Dianthus

(Carnation, Pink)
Growing carnations for show requires dedication and a heated greenhouse. Garden pinks, on the other hand, are relatively easy to grow provided you can give them good soil and full sun. There are many varieties but 'Mrs Sinkins' remains a firm favourite with its wonderful musky scent. 'Hayton White' and 'Houndspool Ruby' are two modern pinks of merit.

Digitalis

(Foxglove)
Imposing plants for the large herbaceous border, foxgloves are biennials that seed themselves freely. Some gardeners will not tolerate them on this account. The most commonly grown are the *D. purpurea* Excelsior Hybrids that carry long spikes of flowers, white, pink or purple. The seeds are poisonous.

Erigeron

(Fleabane)
E. karvinskianus is often found growing down walls and on paving. It has small daisy-like flowers, that open white and then turn to pink and purple as they grow older.

Eryngium

(Sea holly)
Useful and attractive garden perennials, the two varieties most commonly grown are *E. bourgatii*, bluish purple flowerheads, and *E. giganteum*, Miss Willmott's ghost, a startling plant, especially seen in the late evening, that has pale blue flowerheads surrounded by silver white bracts.

Hemerocallis

(Day lily)
Easy-to-grow plants that carry a succession of flowers throughout the

summer. There are many varieties usually found in varying shades of yellow or orange.

Hibiscus

Deciduous or evergreen shrubs, the most commonly grown species are *H. sinosyriacus* and *H. syriacus* and their varieties that are fully hardy and tolerate temperatures down to -15° C (5°F). They have vividly coloured flowers in late summer, often marked in the centre. They need a long hot summer to flower well.

Humulus lupulus

(Hop)

A perennial climber with light green leaves and spikes of green then reddish coloured flowers in summer. These are fragrant. The most commonly grown variety is *H. l.* 'Aureus' which has golden leaves.

Hydrangea

Very popular garden shrubs that flourish in a variety of soil conditions. Varieties of the common hydrangea, *H. macrophylla*, are split into two groups, 'mophead (hortensia)' hydrangeas and 'lacecap', these describe the shape of the flowerheads. Generally the flowers are pink, purple, blue or white, but the colour is affected by the acidity of the soil. Another popular hydrangea is *H.*

petiolaris, the climbing hydrangea, a vigorous climber that prefers a certain amount of shade. It needs restraining unless you have a large wall to cover.

Lavatera

(Mallow)

Mallows either come as large annuals growing up to 1.2 m (4 ft) with large pink flowers, or as semi-evergreen sub-shrubs covered with a profusion of soft pink flowers from late summer through to the autumn. 'Barnsley' has pale pink flowers with red centres, 'Kew Rose' is bright pink.

61

summer

LATE SUMMER

JOBS FOR THE MONTH

The flower and shrub garden

- Water hardy fuchsias every evening, this encourages them to flower. Take cuttings either to increase your stock or to raise plants that you can then exchange with other gardeners.
- Sow seeds of hardy annuals out of doors for flowering early next summer. These include, poppies, cornflowers, love-in-a-mist (nigella), larkspur and scabious. Mark where the seeds have been sown.
- Take cuttings of any pelargoniums and also take cuttings of any evergreen shrubs you want to propagate. Keep them in a shaded cold frame for four to six weeks before planting on.
- Plant any early spring bulbs for flowering next year. These include snowdrops, crocuses, squill, hardy cyclamen, winter aconites and chionodoxa.

Lychnis
(Campion, ragged robin, rose campion)
A popular genus of hardy perennial plants that includes *L. flos-cuculi*, ragged robin with bluish-green leaves and pink, sometimes white, flowers, *L. chalcedonica*, Jerusalem cross, has red flowers and *L. coronaria*, rose campion, grey foliage and bright purple flowers.

Nicotiana
(Tobacco plant)
Grown as annuals for their heavy scent. *N. sylvestrisis* is the most strongly scented. *N. x sanderae* and its varieties has flowers of several colours that remain open all day unlike the species plant where the flowers open only in the evening.

Pelargonium
(Geranium)
A large genus of evergreen perennials and shrubs that are all frost tender and grown as bedding plants in this country. There are six horticultural groups: angel, ivy-leaved, regal, scented-leaved, unique and zonal. Zonal pelargoniums are further divided into six sub-groups. The flowers are usually pink, white or red. Pelargoniums are easy to overwinter given the protection of a cool greenhouse and can be propagated by softwood cuttings in the spring.

Agapanthus Headbourne Hybrids

Perovskia
(Russian sage)
An attractive deciduous shrub or sub-shrub that has salvia-like blue flowers in late summer and silver grey-green thin leaves. The most commonly grown variety is *P.* 'Blue Spire'.

Phlox
A diverse genus of perennials, the most commonly grown are the *P. paniculata* varieties that carry large flowers grouped on conical heads; among the best are 'Amethyst', violet, 'Fujiyama', white and 'Mother-of-Pearl', white with pink tints. *P. stolonifera*, creeping phlox, is low-growing and a good plant for the front of the border or a rock garden. It prefers acid soil.

Phlox subulata 'Scarlet Flame'

Salvia forsskaolii

Salvia
(Sage)

A large and varied genus containing over 900 species of annuals, perennials and shrubs. Some garden favourites are *S. cacaliifolia*, deep blue, *S. coccinea*, red, *S. farinacea*, mealy sage, blue, *S. sclarea,* clary, mauvish pinky-white, (the variety *turkestanica* is the one most often grown), and *S. splendens*, scarlet.

Senecio

A number of senecios have recently been reclassified as brachyglottis, a most unattractive name. They are chiefly grown for their silver-grey coloured foliage.

Solanum
(Potato vine)

The relative of the common potato is a spectacular climbing plant. The two best known varieties are *S. jasminoides,* with fragrant white flowers, and *S. crispum* 'Glasnevin', with lovely soft purple flowers. They are not fully hardy.

Tropaeolum speciosum
(Flame creeper, Scottish flame flower)

A relative of the commonly grown nasturtium, this climber may be difficult to establish. It likes shade and peaty soil. Once established it is a spectacular sight and scrambles through shrubs and over hedges. It flowers in late summer.

Yucca

A strongly architectural plant that, when established, has large spikes of white flowers. Some species are not fully hardy. *Y. filamentosa*, Adam's needle, is the species most commonly grown.

Salvia fulgens

63

JOBS FOR THE MONTH

The greenhouse

- Feed greenhouse tomatoes and potted plants.
- Plant prepared hyacinth bulbs for flowering at Christmas as soon as these become available.

Autumn

EARLY AUTUMN

As summer ends the first hints of autumn arrive. The days shorten, slowly at first, and then with increasing speed. Leaves start to change colour and, if the year is very dry, they may even start to drop. But early autumn is a delightful month in the garden.

The flower that symbolises early autumn in the garden more than any other is the dahlia. Many gardeners have dedicated dahlia beds that brighten the whole garden until they are cut down by the first frosts of autumn, others plant tubers in the herbaceous border. The number and variety available is enormous and they come in a multitude of colours. There are other plants that flower now: Michaelmas daisies bloom and the stonecrop, *Sedum spectabile*, that is so attractive to tortoiseshell and red admiral butterflies. Many lilies are still beautiful and the lovely shrub, the hydrangea, is seen at its best. Japanese anemones are another autumn favourite that flower early.

In the kitchen garden some of the major fruits of the gardener's labours are available. Maincrop potatoes can be lifted, carrots, beetroot and runner beans can be harvested as can the autumn raspberries, which taste almost as good as the summer-fruiting varieties. Blackberries ripen and can be picked and frozen or baked and eaten with the first cooking apples of the year.

Early autumn is probably the best time of year for the gardener to start making major changes to the design and shape of the garden. It is the ideal time to prepare a new lawn and if the soil is moist enough then it is a good time to move any large trees or shrubs that are in the wrong position. If the soil is dry and the weather fine, then delay this for another few weeks until the rains of autumn have really arrived.

Anemone × hybrida 'Königin Charlotte'

THE FLOWERS AND SHRUBS OF ...

JOBS FOR THE MONTH

The fruit and vegetable garden

- Lift onions as they ripen.
- Cover any lettuces if frost threatens.
- Grease band fruit trees to protect them from winter moths crawling up the trees.
- Plant spring cabbages.
- Earth up leeks and celery.
- Blanch endives by covering them with a pot or slate.
- If you wish you can sow a green crop, such as clover, to dig in next spring to raise the nitrogen level of your soil.
- Lift and store maincrop potatoes and carrots.
- Pick outdoor tomatoes as they ripen and if you have a surplus make some green tomato chutney.

Fuchsia magellanica

Abelia x grandiflora

An evergreen or semi-evergreen shrub that carries tubular, white flowers tinged with pink. These are slightly fragrant. The plant has small, glossy, green oval leaves carried on arching branches. It is a useful shrub for gardens with clay soil, and can make a hedge in mild areas.

Anemone

(Japanese anemone)
One of the most popular autumn-flowering perennials, Japanese anemones come in a variety of colours from white through pink to red. There is a considerable number available to the gardener but among the most popular are *A.* x *hybrida* 'Honorine Jobert', white, and *A.* x *h.* 'Königin Charlotte', semi-double pink. They like some shade.

Calluna vulgaris

(Ling, Scottish heather)
The native heather that turns the hills of Scotland purple in late summer is a useful garden plant for ground-cover and is also attractive to bees. It requires acid soil to flourish. There is a large number of varieties available, many with yellow leaves that retain their interest throughout the winter. The varieties *C. v.* 'Kinlochruel' and 'My Dream' have white flowers.

Dahlia

There are ten groups of dahlias, known by their flower shapes, a number of sub-groups, and to round it off, the main groups, such as ball and cactus, are further divided into six sizes from giant to miniature. Dahlias are a world of their own and there are over 20,000 varieties available for the gardener to choose from. Tubers should be planted out in the spring and lifted and stored when flowering is over and the first frosts of the autumn have blackened the foliage. Their beautiful showy flowers are usually in various shades of pink, orange, red, yellow and white.

Echinops

(The globe thistle)
Useful plants for the herbaceous border where their pale colours are a foil for other more vivid plants, globe thistles have round ball-like white, grey, or blue flowerheads held upright on slender stalks. *E. bannaticus* 'Taplow Blue' has bright blue flowerheads and *E. ritro* 'Veitch's Blue', darker blue.

Dahlia

Eucryphia x nymansensis 'Nymansay'

A small upright evergreen tree that carries pure white flowers in late summer or early autumn. While eucryphia generally prefer acid soil, this variety will tolerate alkaline soil. It likes its roots to be in shade and may need some protection in very hard winters.

Fuchsia

A large genus of plants that can be treated as hardy in mild and coastal areas. Hardy fuchsias make a good informal hedge. Most hardy fuchsias are varieties bred from *F. magellanica* and there are a number of red, white, pink and mixed colours. Both hardy and tender fuchsias make attractive small shrubs flowering in late summer and early autumn.

Galtonia

(Summer hyacinth)
Bulbous perennials that flower late in summer with thick, strap-shaped leaves and heads of white-drooping bells that are slightly scented. There are pale green markings at the base of each petal. They like a sunny site and self-seed freely.

Scabiosa

(Pincushion flower, scabious)
Attractive flowers, mainly lilac, mauve and white, that bloom for long periods from late summer onwards in borders or wild areas of the garden. 'Miss Willmott' is the best white variety.

Tamarix

(Tamarisk)
This is a useful shrub for gardens where there is little frost and for coastal areas. *T. ramosissima* tolerates salt spray and carries a profusion of pink flowers on arching spikes in late summer and early autumn.

EARLY AUTUMN

The flower and shrub garden

- If you are planning to make a new lawn this is the time to prepare and level the site. This applies whether you are planning to sow grass seed or lay turf.
- Check on your climbing and rambler roses, prune if needed and tie in any new shoots.
- Check also any cuttings that you have taken earlier in the year and pull out and throw away any that have failed to strike.
- Lift and divide border irises if they have become overcrowded and not flowered well. Irises like well-drained soil and a sunny position to flower at their best. They also like to have their rhizomes baked by the sun so cut back the leaves by half when they have finished flowering.
- Cut the leaves of the winter-flowering iris, *Iris unguicularis*, in half. This will encourage the production of more flowers.
- Take cuttings of plants such as pelargoniums, fuchsias, penstemons and anthemis.
- When summer bedding plants start to die back, start clearing the beds, fork over the soil, add fertiliser and prepare the site for winter-flowering plants such as pansies.
- Check your lawn and repair any worn areas by sowing new seed or cutting out and patching with new turf.
- Towards the end of the month start planting all new trees and shrubs so that they can become established before the winter. Autumn is much the best time to plant shrubs and bare-root roses, and any planted now will make far better plants than container-grown plants planted in the spring.
- Finish planting any early spring-flowering bulbs that were not planted last month and start planting daffodils and narcissi for next spring. These will flower better if they are planted now rather than later.
- Plant lily bulbs if these are available.
- If you want to make a rock garden, now is a good time of the year to establish one and put in new plants.
- Plant border pinks and carnations.
- Start sweeping up the leaves from the trees when they begin to fall, the easiest way to collect leaves is with a rotary lawnmower. This also helps to break them down so that they become compost more quickly.
- Root cuttings of hardier plants in a cold frame, but pelargonium cuttings require a minimum temperature of 7°C (45°F) over the winter months. If you are taking pelargonium cuttings leave them to dry for 12 hours before potting up. They then form a callous and are less likely to rot.

MAKING A

Every garden, however small, should have a lawn. There is a garden designer-led trend to do away with lawns, and it is considered chic in some quarters to cover the lawn area with gravel or paving. There may be a case in very small town gardens, when a lawn is impractical and the back garden should be paved, but conversely the benefits of a lawn are even greater in a town when the eye can rest on the cool green expanse after a day sitting in an office or walking on concrete pavements.

The type of lawn you have or aspire to must depend very much on your own circumstances. If there are young children who are going to use the lawn as a football or cricket pitch then you must sow some tough rye

JOBS FOR THE MONTH

The greenhouse
- Check that your greenhouse heater is working properly.
- Clean off the greenhouse summer shading ready for the winter.
- Bring in any house plants and greenhouse plants that have spent the summer out of door.
- Plant hyacinth bulbs that you are planning to have flowering indoors during the winter. Keep them in the dark for six weeks or so until they have formed good root systems.
- Repot any cacti if this is necessary. Make a band of paper to hold spiky varieties while you do this.

NEW LAWN

grass that will survive some hard treatment. If you do not have the pleasure of a young family then you can try and achieve a sward of bowling-green-type perfection and sow only the finest grass seed.

If you are planning to renew the lawn in your garden or plant a lawn then the two times of the year for this are early spring and autumn. Autumn is the better of the two choices and gives you the best chance of preparing the site thoroughly. The first thing to do is to spray the whole area with a systemic weed killer such as Roundup, to kill off all existing grasses and weeds. When all the growth has died, dig over the site, level it, add plenty of garden compost or gravel to assist drainage of the lawn, remove as many stones and pebbles as you can and tread it firm. When the soil is firm all over, rake and roll the lawn, levelling the soil as required until the time comes to sow.

Sow the seed carefully scattering it in one direction and then in another. Some people are politically a touch incorrect and add peat to the topsoil when sowing. This does assist the establishment of the fine grass roots and peat substitute can be used instead. If it doesn't rain soon after you have sown your new lawn, water very carefully with a fine hose to assist germination, but avoid this if you can as watering disturbs the even application of the seed.

The other way of making a lawn is to lay turf. This is much more expensive than sowing seed and you have to take care to keep the new lawn watered, especially in periods of drought. It is a good idea to use turf

to repair any worn edges of the lawn in the spring, although very often you can do this by cutting out a piece of turf from the lawn and relaying it.

Lawn Hints and Tips

Always buy the right sort of lawnmower for the lawn you require. If you have a lot of grass you will need a sit on mower that can cut a large area of grass quickly; if you want bowling green perfection you will need a cylinder mower; if you have a certain amount of rough grass you will need a robust rotary mower.

Lawns should be treated in the same way as plants. They need to be weeded and fertilised. Apply a combined weed-and-feed granule or spray in the autumn and lawn sand in the spring to help to control any moss. Selective weed killers can be applied through the summer in either a liquid or a granular form.

Lawns need to be mowed frequently – at least once a week in the summer and probably more in late spring when the grass is growing strongly. However don't cut the grass too short as this damages the roots.

Other things to heed are: drainage – if the lawn is poorly drained then moss will grow; scarifying or raking to improve the grass; and watering, although lawns do recover remarkably quickly after even the longest drought.

MID AUTUMN

Although the flowers in the garden become fewer and fewer, the middle of autumn is, for many, one of the most charming times of the year. As the flowers fade, the leaves of many trees and shrubs become brilliantly tinted, some of them bear brightly coloured fruits and a number have brightly coloured bark. It is worthwhile for every gardener to plant even just one or two trees or shrubs for the brilliant autumn colour that they provide. Among the best autumn shrubs for leaf colour is *Fothergilla major*, while the leaves of the Japanese maples, acers, turn red and purple, and the Mountain ash, or native rowan, has clusters of coloured berries to go with delicately coloured leaves.

Early and mid autumn mark the beginning of the gardener's year. Now is the time for planning, and the weather will usually allow a good deal of work to be done outside, both routine clearing up and major reconstruction tasks, such as preparing the site for a new lawn or constructing a rock garden. This is the time of the year when it is best to plant new evergreens. Evergreens require much more care in planting than deciduous shrubs or trees because their leaves need constant nourishment from the roots and if conditions are adverse then it is difficult for the roots to become established quickly enough. If they are planted now, when the days are shortening and growth is slowing, the soil is still warm enough for the roots to become established. This does not only apply to evergreens, many trees and shrubs are much better if they are planted in the autumn and it is particularly true of roses that should be planted as bare-root specimens in this month if you can arrange supply from the nursery. Planted now they will make much better plants than those planted in the spring.

Colchicum speciosum 'Album'

THE FLOWERS AND SHRUBS OF ...

JOBS FOR THE MONTH

The fruit and vegetable garden

- Take cuttings of any fruit bushes that you wish to propagate.
- Prune raspberries, loganberries, blackcurrants and blackberries.
- Plant spring cabbages if this has not been done before.
- Start clearing and digging the vegetable garden, especially if you have heavy soil that is difficult to work when it is very wet and waterlogged.
- Pick and store apples and pears.
- Lift potatoes, carrots and beetroot and store them in a cool dry place. Parsnips should be left in the ground and dug when required.

JOBS FOR THE MONTH

The greenhouse

- Take in some summer bedding plants and keep them over winter, they will provide sufficient cuttings for the following year.
- Pot up any prepared bulbs for flowering indoors during the winter. These include hyacinths, daffodils, narcissi and crocuses.

Aster

(Michaelmas daisy)
Popular hardy herbaceous perennials that start flowering in early autumn. They are tolerant of most garden conditions. The commonest garden Michaelmas daisies are A. *novae-angliae* and A. *novi-belgii* and their varieties and the plants are available in a wide range of colours from blue, purple and yellow, to pink and white.

Ceanothus (Autumn flowering)

(Californian lilac)
Most people think of ceanothus as spring-flowering shrubs, but there are a number of varieties that flower in the autumn, C. 'Autumnal Blue' is an evergreen shrub with sky-blue flowers and C. 'Gloire de Versailles' has paler blue flowers carried in large sprays sometimes as long as 10 cm (4 in).

Ceratostigma

Attractive low-growing ground-covering plants, the best-known species are C. *plumbaginoides*, a spreading perennial, that has blue flowers in autumn and foliage that turns a brilliant red, and C. *willmottianum*, a spreading deciduous shrub, with lighter blue flowers and red autumn foliage.

Colchicum

(Meadow saffron)
Charming bulbs that flower in the autumn and are often, wrongly, referred to as autumn crocus. C. *autumnale*, has crocus-like pink flowers in autumn, other varieties are deeper pink, yellow or white. The leaves appear after the flowers and last until midsummer.

Nerine bowdenii

(Guernsey lily)
Bulbous perennials that have decorative sprays of pink and white flowers in the autumn. They used to be considered greenhouse plants only, but they are perfectly hardy given the protection of a south- or south-west-facing wall. They prefer sandy soil.

Persicaria affinis

(Knotweed)
A dense ground-covering perennial with pink to red flowers on upright spikes that flowers from midsummer. In the autumn the leaves of P. *affinis* turn a brilliant red.

Sedum

(Stonecrop)
Sedums can be both deciduous or evergreen perennials. The most popular garden varieties are S. 'Herbstfreude', previously called

'Autumn Joy', with flat heads of pinkish flowers that turn red and golden in autumn and S. 'Ruby Glow', another deciduous perennial with deeper red flowers. They are very attractive to butterflies and should be grown in any garden where you want to see these insects on the plants.

Viburnum opulus
(Guelder rose)
A justly popular shrub that carries large white elder-like flowers in spring and red or orange berries in autumn. The leaves are carried on greenish-red stalks and turn red or orange in autumn.

JOBS FOR THE MONTH

The flower and shrub garden
- If you are making a new lawn lay turf or sow seed now (see page 71).
- Apply autumn food and weedkiller to the lawn.
- Move any shrubs that you have marked as being in the wrong place in the garden. Water the plant, dig out a large hole and take as much of the root system of the shrub, plus the soil, as possible. Trim any damaged roots and then replant in a prepared site adding leafmould or garden compost. Water if the weather has been dry.

- Divide large herbaceous plants.
- Take cuttings of evergreen shrubs.
- Take cuttings of roses and prepare a bed for them.
- Lift and store tuberous summer and autumn flowering plants when their flowering season is over. These include dahlias, gladioli and begonias.
- If you have a pond, now is the time to thin out any water plants that have grown too vigorously and move any tender aquatic plants to the greenhouse.
- Continue planting, particularly if the weather has been reasonably mild.

Conifers, evergreens, evergreen hedges, clematis and climbing shrubs, such as *Hydrangea petiolaris*, wisteria, ornamental vines and summer jasmine can all be planted at this time of year.
- Plant out any summer biennials such as foxgloves, that you may have raised from seed.
- Plant pansies and primulas for a winter flowering display.
- Plant out wallflowers in the position where they will flower next year.
- Plant out daffodils and narcissi bulbs if you did not manage to do this last month.

autumn MID AUTUMN

LATE AUTUMN

Flowering plants are now over for the year and, although some flowers remain, the next plants that come into flower are the first flowers of the new year. Most of the deciduous trees will lose their leaves during this month, and, while the trees that still carry leaves are often colourful, there is the feeling that one good autumn gale or one severe frost will remove the remaining colour from the garden. It is the time of year to enjoy the sight of the last berries on the trees and hedges and to marvel at the colour of the crab apples before the birds and squirrels take them for their winter hordes.

Nevertheless, late autumn marks the start of the gardening year and in this respect is a continuation of the preceding month. The only warning is one of weather, for, as winter draws in, rain and frost become more frequent and the garden becomes a much less inviting place than earlier in the year. If there are no major garden alterations planned then jobs can wait a week, or even two or three, if the weather is adverse and outside work is impossible.

When the weather is fine then much can be done. Vacant ground can be dug over and manure or compost added to it. This is also the best time of the year to add lime to the soil. This is particularly effective if you garden on heavy clay as the lime helps to combine with the superfine particles of clay soil into larger particles that are more easily cultivated. Don't manure land to which you have added lime, and scatter the lime on the surface of the soil and let the weather wash it in. It is also the time of year to start raking up all the leaves as they fall from the trees and adding them to the compost heap or making a dedicated pile of leafmould. This is excellent to use for planting and also helps the composition of the soil but leaves take longer to break down than ordinary garden compost.

Acer pseudoplatanus 'Brilliantissimum'

THE FLOWERS AND SHRUBS OF ...

JOBS FOR THE MONTH

The fruit and vegetable garden

- Dig over any vacant ground and add compost. Leave the compost on the surface of the soil and it will be incorporated by worms and weather. Leave the soil in rough clods and this will help the weathering.
- Lime any heavy clay soils in rotation. Test the pH of the soil before you do this as too much lime locks vitamins into the soil that plants need for growth.
- Start pruning apple and pear trees and spray them against pests. Plum trees should be pruned in summer.
- Sow seeds of broad beans. Broad beans sown in the autumn are far less prone to blackfly than those sown in the spring.

JOBS FOR THE MONTH

The greenhouse

- Clean the greenhouse and insulate it against winter frosts. Clear bubble wrap makes the best insulation and you can get special clips to hold it in place.
- Bring in chrysanthemums and tender fuchsias.
- Take chrysanthemum cuttings when the plants have finished flowering.
- Prune the greenhouse vine if you have one.

Acer
(Maple)
Nearly all the acers have wonderful autumn colour. The most vivid belongs to A. palmatum, the Japanese maple, and its varieties, that turns shades of yellow, orange, gold and crimson.

Cotinus
(Smoke bush)
Another shrub or small tree grown largely for its autumn colour. The young foliage may be green, purple or bronze, depending on the variety grown, but they all turn brilliant orange or red in the autumn.

Euonymus
(Spindle)
A useful genus of shrubs, the most commonly grown are varieties of E. fortunei, the spindle tree. The leaves are evergreen and heavily marked with gold and silver. E. europaeus 'Red Cascade' is a deciduous shrub with dark green leaves that turn rich scarlet in autumn followed by large quantities of red berries.

Fothergilla major
A slow-growing deciduous shrub that carries small, white, scented bottle-brush type flowers in spring and whose leaves turn brilliant yellow, orange and purple before the winter frosts. They dislike lime and prefer a sheltered position in the garden.

Gleditsia triacanthos
(Honey locust)
A fast-growing deciduous tree with leaves that turn a brilliant yellow in autumn. The variety 'Sunburst' also has yellow leaves in the spring and is the most frequently grown.

Liquidamber styraciflua
(Sweet gum)
Another tree well-known for the brilliant colour of its autumn leaves. These are maple-like and mid green when they emerge in spring. They are often grown as specimen trees .

Liriodendron tulipifera
(Tulip tree)
A large vigorous tree with distinctly shaped, square-tipped leaves. It carries cup-shaped greenish flowers in summer and in the autumn the leaves turn a bright golden-yellow.

late

Gleditsia triacanthos 'Sunburst'

Rhus typhina

(Stag's horn sumach)
An upright suckering deciduous shrub grown mainly for its large leaves that turn orange-yellow in autumn. The shrub has reddish-brown flower spikes that last through the winter.

Sorbus

(Mountain ash)
One of the best trees for the smaller garden where it makes an ideal specimen. The leaves are generally pale green and turn yellow and orange in autumn when the small creamy-white flowers of summer bear clusters of berries in white, yellow, orange or red, depending on the variety grown. These berries are very popular with birds and seldom last long on the tree.

Vitis coignetiae

(Crimson glory vine)
A vine grown not for its grapes, which are inedible, but for its foliage that turns a brilliant red in autumn. It is one of the best foliage climbers and clings by way of its tendrils.

JOBS FOR THE MONTH

The flower and shrub garden

- Plant any trees and shrubs not planted the previous month. Prepare the ground thoroughly and stake any young trees to prevent windrock. Place the stake away from the tree in the direction of the prevailing wind. Label all new plants clearly otherwise you may well forget what you have planted.
- Apply autumn weedkiller and feed to the lawn if this has not been done before.
- If you wish, start to tidy and clear the herbaceous border although you can leave this in place and clear the border next spring. The dead foliage provides some cover for insects for the birds and any tender plants and looks attractive when rimmed with frost on cold winter's mornings.
- Take cuttings of any shrubs that you wish to propagate.
- Protect any tender plants and shrubs from the frosts to come.
- Move any plants in the herbaceous border that are in the wrong position, but be sure that you know exactly where everything is as otherwise you may dig up plants that have died down and you wish to retain.

autumn

LATE AUTUMN

Winter

EARLY WINTER

This is the time of the year when the last leaves of the old year disappear and the first flowers of the new year appear: these include *Viburnum tinus*, laurustinus, *Hamamelis mollis*, witch hazel, and the first of the winter-flowering heathers. All plants that flower at this time of the year are subject to the weather, and if it has been unseasonably cold or warm then the time between flowering may vary by up to four weeks from year to year within the same garden. This also applies to winter-flowering bulbs: the first snowdrops in a garden may emerge at any time between late December and early February. There is great satisfaction to be obtained from the early flowers in a garden, and the fact that there are so few makes their appearance all the more welcome.

If weather permits it is a time for tidying and planting, pruning and repairing. Paths and fences can be examined and repaired and, if the weather is really kind, it is not too late to plan and plant a herbaceous border, although this project may have to be abandoned if the ground becomes too heavy to work comfortably. This can be a difficult thing to accomplish successfully as the gardener has to take into account the ultimate size of the plant as well as the colour and flowering season. One of the best resolutions any gardener can make is to acknowledge all mistakes and move any plant that is found growing in the wrong place. Inevitably this is easiest in the summer months when the plants are in full colour, but it is better if they can be marked carefully and moved in late autumn or early winter.

Elaeagnus commutata

THE FLOWERS AND SHRUBS OF ...

JOBS FOR THE MONTH

The fruit and vegetable garden

- Continue digging when weather conditions permit.
- At the end of the period prepare beds and plant shallots. It was a country tradition that these were planted on the shortest day of the year.
- Lift leeks and parsnips as required.
- Continue pruning fruit trees, particularly any apricot trees if you have them. These must be pruned when they are dormant.
- Test your soil and, if the Ph is less than 6.5, add lime on the surface according to the manufacturer's instructions. Do not add any compost or manure when you lime. Liming can be done at any time, but autumn and early winter are the most suitable months.

JOBS FOR THE MONTH

The flower and shrub garden

- Top dress the lawn with sand if you garden on heavy soil to improve drainage and the quality of the grass.
- Complete any garden tasks that you have not managed to complete in the last two months.
- Sweep up the last of the autumn leaves and add them to your compost heap.
- Sow seeds of rock plants and put them out of doors in boxes in a bed of ash.
- Prune roses. Opinions differ as to the best time to prune roses but many are coming round to the opinion that they should be pruned in the winter when the plants are dormant.
- Tidy up the compost heap and turn it over to keep the decomposition even.
- Plan out a new herbaceous border and start digging out and preparing the site. Add manure or garden compost to improve the condition of the soil.

Cornus alba 'Sibirica'
(Red-barked dogwood)
This is the dogwood grown for the colour of its bark in winter. Cut it back hard in the spring to promote new young growth.

Elaeagnus
A genus of mainly evergreen shrubs grown for their silver and gold marked leaves. They are a colourful addition to the garden all the year and many have small scented flowers in autumn. Among the most commonly grown is E. x ebbingei 'Gilt Edge' with dark green leaves and prominent yellow margins.

Malus
(Crab apple)
Crab apples, as opposed to M. x domestica, eating apples, are grown as ornamental trees and shrubs for their profuse fruit, usually red or gold in autumn, and their flowers in spring. 'John Downie' is one of the best varieties with red fruit, 'Golden Hornet' has golden yellow fruit.

early

Pyracantha
(Firethorn)
Evergreen spiky shrubs that are often grown on north walls although they prefer partial shade or sun. They have white flowers in early summer and in the autumn the shrubs are covered with red, yellow or orange berries according to the variety grown.

Sarcococca humilis
(Sweet box, Christmas box)
A small evergreen shrub that has glossy foliage and white, pink-tinged fragrant flowers in winter.

Viburnum farreri syn. V. fragrans
An upright shrub that has dark green leaves, turning red in autumn, and very fragrant pink flowers carried on bare branches in winter through to early spring.

JOBS FOR THE MONTH

The greenhouse
- Check winter-flowering bulbs and bring them into the light when they are 3–5 cm (1–2 in) high.
- Get all your tools, such as secateurs and shears, sharpened professionally.
- Water plants sparingly. It is better to underwater in winter than overwater.

- Check that your maximum/minimum thermometer is working properly.
- Ventilate the greenhouse on sunny days.
- Check on any bulbs and tubers that you are storing over winter and discard any that show signs of rot. Do this every month.

winter

EARLY WINTER

MIDWINTER

It is probably true that gardens are visited less often in the middle of winter than at any other time of the year. There is, inevitably, little to see and often the weather conspires to keep the gardener indoors. But for the gardener who ventures out there is an increasing number of plants coming into flower. The hellebores start to bloom and the laurustinus flowers develop while the yellow flowers of the winter jasmine brighten many a wall. The Algerian iris, *Iris unguicularis*, flowers, and the very first snowdrops may appear together with the yellow winter aconites, while buds start to swell on many of the fruit trees.

It may be repetitious to say so, but work out of doors depends very much on the weather. If possible, then, the kitchen garden can be dug and manured and fruit trees should be pruned and sprayed against pests in the coming year. However, for the gardener lucky enough to possess a heated greenhouse, there are many jobs that can be done and much colour to be seen. Cyclamen, primulas, hyacinths and narcissi planted in pots and kept in a heated environment will all be in flower, and the first seeds can be sown of sweet peas, antirrhinums, cannas, chrysanthemums and hollyhocks. Make sure that you have sufficient room in your greenhouse if you plan to sow a number of seeds as they will all need pricking out and have to be given light and shelf room.

Finally if you do have a heavy fall of snow, make sure that you take a photograph of the garden covered in its winter coat and then knock off the snow from the branches of all trees and shrubs that may break under the weight.

Jasminum nudiflorum

THE FLOWERS AND SHRUBS OF ...

JOBS FOR THE MONTH

The fruit and vegetable garden and greenhouse

- Finish pruning and spraying fruit trees.
- Plan the kitchen garden for the coming year.
- Start sowing seeds in the greenhouse if you can offer them some heat.
- This is the time of year, when the weather is very inclement, to give the greenhouse a thorough cleaning. Wash and disinfect all your pots and seed trays. Scrub the staging and check through all the seeds left over from last year and throw away any that are out of date. Make a list of all the new seeds you need to buy.

Clematis cirrhosa

Evergreen, early-flowering clematis that has yellow four-petalled cup-shaped flowers from midwinter onwards; var. *balearica* has yellow fragrant flowers, speckled red-brown, and 'Freckles' has creamy pink flowers, speckled with red.

Erica

(Winter-flowering heather)
Many heathers flower in winter. *E. carnea* and *E. x darleyensis* are the main species and they are followed by *E. arborea*, the tree heather or heath, in early spring. They prefer acid soil and full sun although some heathers will tolerate alkaline soil. Clip them after flowering to keep the plants tidy.

Hamamelis

(Witch hazel)
Deciduous trees with good autumn colour and tortuous, fragrant, spider-shaped flowers born on bare branches in winter. *H. mollis*, the Chinese witch hazel, has golden-yellow flowers, varieties of *H. x intermedia*, have flowers ranging in colour from yellow through to gold and red.

Helleborus argutifolius

(Corsican hellebore)
Formerly called *H. corsicus*, this well-known evergreen has long dark green leaves and in the winter vivid green flowers with yellow stamens that last for several months. They like neutral soil and some shade.

Jasminum nudiflorum

(Winter jasmine)
One of the first flowering shrubs of the year, winter jasmine has clear yellow flowers carried on arching stems from midwinter onwards. The leaves appear after the flowers are over. The shrub is usually grown against a wall and will require support.

Mahonia

Mahonias are a fairly large genus of shrubs with around 70 species. They are good plants for the winter garden as the varieties of *M. aquifolium* have striking leaves that turn wonderful shades of red, orange and purple in the autumn and winter, while *M. lomariifolia* and *M. x media* have long upright racemes of deliciously scented yellow flowers from late autumn onwards.

mid

Viburnum tinus

(Laurustinus)

One of the best shrubs that merits a
place in all gardens. It is compact,
fairly slow-growing, evergreen and has
attractive fragrant clusters of flowers
from early winter right through to the
spring. There are a number of
varieties of which the best known are
probably 'Eve Price', with pinkish
flowers, and 'Gwenllian' with darker
pink buds and pinkish-white flowers.

JOBS FOR THE MONTH

The flower and shrub garden

•   Order seeds, summer bulbs and
    shrubs for delivery in the spring
    of next year.

•   Look at your garden plan and
    see whether you wish to make
    any alterations.

•   Knock any heavy snow off shrubs
    and trees as it can damage
    branches and spoil the shape.

•   Check on the protection that
    you can offer any half-hardy
    shrubs you are growing. Wrap
    them in polythene or cover with
    straw and sacking.

winter MIDWINTER

LATE WINTER

Within the limited number of hours that are available at this time of year a surprisingly large number of garden jobs can be started or accomplished. Gardening in the first months of the year depends entirely on the weather. If there are weeks of frost and snow then nothing can be done, and in the same way if there is constant rain the gardener will often do more harm than good if much work is attempted. If the weather is extremely adverse then it is better to do nothing, rather than compact the soil by trying to cultivate water-logged ground. Don't worry if gardening proves virtually impossible, you can always catch up later.

In spite of this it is a time of the year when the gardener finds much of interest. Conditions permitting, shrubs and trees can be planted, if they have not been planted in the autumn, the vegetable garden can be dug and prepared for sowing in the coming months, bulbs start to appear and the first flowers of the year arrive.

A surprising number of flowers bloom in late winter. Chief among them, of course, are the snowdrops and winter aconites that make such a lovely contrast of yellow and white when they appear together. However those who garden on the western side of the country will often have difficulty growing aconites with any degree of success – they like alkaline soil. The strawberry tree, *Arbutus unedo*, and the lovely mimosa, *Acacia dealbata*, are in flower although they will probably only survive in the warmer parts of the country, the Cornelian cherry, *Cornus mas*, is covered in yellow flowers and the winter-flowering iris, *Iris unguicularis*, comes into bloom.

Helleborus niger

THE FLOWERS AND SHRUBS OF ...

JOBS FOR THE MONTH

The flower and shrub garden

- Start clearing the herbaceous border, remove any weeds, fork it over lightly and add mulch or garden compost when you have finished.
- Prune hybrid tea and floribunda roses if this has not been done earlier. Note there is considerable division of opinion about the best time to prune roses. Many gardeners will wait until later in the spring, others like to prune in late autumn or even in midwinter when the plants are dormant. It is probably advisable not to prune roses during a mild spell in winter as growth will start that may well die back when the frosts of spring return.
- If the weather is suitable, plant any trees, shrubs and climbers left unplanted from last autumn to give them as long a growing season as possible.
- Tidy and repair any garden paths and the edges of borders.
- Start digging out a new herbaceous border if you are planning one.
- Check and protect plants from frost.

Daphne mezereum
(Mezereon)
The best-known of a popular genus of shrubs, the mezereon flowers in late winter and carries very fragrant, rosy-purple flowers on bare branches. The leaves appear later and the shrub has bright red berries. The variety 'Bowles' Variety' is white with yellow berries.

Eranthis hyemalis
(Winter aconite)
Winter aconites are tubers that prefer alkaline soil that does not dry out in summer. Given these conditions they will colonise freely. They flower with snowdrops and are often grown together in semi-woodland, where the carpets of the small yellow and white flowers are particularly attractive in the early months of the year.

Galanthus
(Snowdrop)
Snowdrops can appear from late December onwards in mild winters, but generally bloom from late January to early February. They used to be called the 'Fair Maids of February'. The best-known varieties are *G. nivalis*, the common snowdrop, and *G. elwesii*, the giant snowdrop, although there are many others. Snowdrops should be planted 'in the green', when they are in leaf after flowering, and are more difficult to establish if grown from bulbs. The clumps should be split every two or three years and replanted.

Helleborus
(Hellebore, Christmas rose, Lenten rose)
Hellebores are one of the joys of the winter garden. The best-known species is *H. niger*, the Christmas rose, with its white flowers, greenish centres and yellow stamens, *H. orientalis*, the Lenten rose, has purple, pink or grey flowers and both *H. argutifolius* syn. *H. corsicus*, the Corsican hellebore, and *H. foetidus*, the stinking hellebore, have green flowers. They prefer, indeed need, some shade.

Lonicera
(Winter-flowering honeysuckle)
Unlike their better-known, summer-flowering, climbing relatives, winter honeysuckles are bushy shrubs that surprisingly flower in midwinter. The best-known are *L. fragrantissima* and *L. standishii*, both of which are semi-evergreen and carry smallish creamy-white fragrant flowers followed by red berries.

late

Eranthis hyemalis

JOBS FOR THE MONTH

The greenhouse
- Take cuttings of chrysanthemums as these become available.
- Start sowing seeds of annuals and hardy border perennials.
- Take cuttings of any summer bedding plants that you have been overwintering in the greenhouse, such as pelargoniums.
- Pot up bulbs of any lilies that you are planning to grow in containers.

Viola x wittrockiana
(Winter-flowering pansies)
These are generally grown as annuals or biennials and are one of the delights of the winter garden. It is easiest to buy pansies from the local nursery and plant them out when they are in flower. Most winter-flowering pansies are varieties of *Viola* x *wittrockiana* and are available in an almost infinite number of colours and varieties.

93

JOBS FOR THE MONTH

The fruit and vegetable garden
- Plant broad beans under cloches.
- Finish digging the kitchen garden and add compost and manure.
- Prepare beds and sow parsnips, onions and shallots.
- Chit seed potatoes: put them in a tray in a cool light room with the ends of the tubers pointing upwards. This should be done about six weeks before you plan to plant them and gives them a better start.

- Put cloches or sheets of clear plastic over any beds you have managed to prepare. This helps to dry and warm the soil and makes cultivation much easier in the spring.
- Cut down autumn-fruiting raspberries to 15 cm (6 in) from the ground.
- Spray peaches and nectarines with Bordeaux mixture to help prevent leaf curl.

winter

LATE WINTER

GARDEN TOOLS

All gardeners are advised to buy the best garden tools that they can afford and to have as large a range of tools available as possible. This may be a counsel perfection but it can save a great deal of time, worry and effort.

Don't forget you will need tools such as a hammer, wire cutters, nails and screwdrivers, as well as the conventional gardening equipment.

ESSENTIAL TOOLS

Lawnmowers
Buy a lawnmower that will enable you to cut all your grass as quickly as possible, however expensive. Also, for the novice gardener, buy a rotary mower rather than a cylinder mower and if you want rolled stripes on the lawn, buy a model that has a roller on the back and not just wheels. Buy a mower that collects the grass, for not only will the lawn look better and be healthier, but you will provide yourself with the basic ingredient for garden compost.

Fork, spades, rakes and hoes
You will need at least one of each. It is useful to have a flat plastic rake to rake up leaves as well as a traditional rake that you will need if you have to prepare beds for sowing vegetables in the kitchen garden. A lawn rake with sprung tines for raking moss from the lawn or raking gravel is also useful. Stainless steel spades make digging easier but they have very sharp edges and slice open the bottoms of gumboots with effortless ease.

Trowels, forks, weeders
You will need one of each. It can help to have two trowels, one with a broad blade, and one with a narrow blade.

Pruning tools
You will need one good pair of secateurs, possibly a pair of loppers, although these may not be essential in a small garden, a pruning saw and a good gardening knife.

Shears
You will need a pair of edging shears to keep the lawn edges neat and a pair of ordinary shears to clip hedges of plants such as lavender.

Wheelbarrow
Buy as big a wheelbarrow as you can and get one with a proper pneumatic tyre at the front, as it is much easier to push when it is full of soil.

Watering cans and sprayers
You really should have two watering cans, one for beneficial watering and one reserved for weedkiller only. You also need a sprayer to spray roses and other plants in the summer. Ideally, you should have two of these, but if you make do with one wash it out thoroughly after use.

NON-ESSENTIAL TOOLS

There are a number of other tools that you may or may not be able to survive without. These include: bulb planters, worth having if you plant a lot of bulbs; dibbers, essential if you are planting out leeks in the garden; cultivating tools, they can be quite useful but you can get by with a fork and a rake; aerators for the lawn, again you can make do with a fork but it is not quite as good or as quick; half-moon edgers, they make a better job of edging a lawn than the slightly curved spade; leaf-sweepers are a waste of money, in my opinion. You can invest as much money as you can afford on sophisticated computer-controlled irrigation systems, if you want, although a hose and sprinkler head is usually enough; garden lines for sowing seeds in a straight line; nylon line trimmers; hedge-cutters; chipper/shredder machines; axe; pickaxe; sledgehammer; rotary cultivator; chainsaw; long-armed tree pruner.

Many of these tools are a great help if you have a large garden and not much manual help. You will also need seed trays, pots, and modular systems – these are a help when sowing and planting seeds under glass.

INDEX

Figures in italics denote illustration